BEST CANADIAN POETRY
2021

BEST
CANADIAN
POETRY

GUEST EDITOR: SOUVANKHAM
THAMMAVONGSA

SERIES EDITOR: ANITA LAHEY

2021

BIBLIOASIS
WINDSOR, ONTARIO

FIRST EDITION
ISBN 978-1-77196-439-5 (Trade Paper)
ISBN 978-1-77196-440-1 (eBook)

Series editor: Anita Lahey
Guest editor: Souvankham Thammavongsa
Editors at Large: Michael Fraser, Laboni Islam, waaseyaa'sin Christine Sy
Copyedited by Emily Donaldson
Cover and text designed by Gordon Robertson

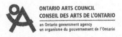

Published with the generous assistance of the Canada Council for the Arts, which last year invested $153 million to bring the arts to Canadians throughout the country, and the financial support of the Government of Canada. Biblioasis also acknowledges the support of the Ontario Arts Council (OAC), an agency of the Government of Ontario, which last year funded 1,709 individual artists and 1,078 organizations in 204 communities across Ontario, for a total of $52.1 million, and the contribution of the Government of Ontario through the Ontario Book Publishing Tax Credit and Ontario Creates.

PRINTED AND BOUND IN CANADA

CONTENTS

FOREWORD

Emergencies of feeling

> *Tell us, they said, no one died*
> — Ronna Bloom, "Is it Safe?"

> *my mother doesn't tell me about the dangerous things*
> — Tina Do, "i tell my mother everything"

> *What do I mean by fear? Why I mean that thing that*
> *drives you to write—*
> — Mary Ruefle, "On Fear"

The first image you'll encounter in the 2021 edition of *Best Canadian Poetry* is a wing. It appears in the title of Eugenia Zuroski's spare poem, "a wing on the pavement, now kept in a jar." By this we know it was worth retrieving. It might be beautiful. It's small enough to fit inside a jar.

Zuroski's poem offers perilous questions about money, poverty; a tremulous assertion that "no, we are fine. we are better than fine"; nervous repetition: "but how," "yes, but how." The lines tremble like fragile wings. That trembling makes sense, for the queries posed in this poem might translate into the awful question, "How do we survive?"

The question mark is mine: none appear in the poem. It's as if Zuroski is pulling back, warding off answers. After all, who among us would dare propose an answer to, "we have negative money / what does that mean"?

You're holding in your hand just fifty of the many hundreds of poems authored by Canadian writers that appeared in periodicals in print or online in 2020, and that were read, and in many cases reread, then reread again, by *BCP*'s guest editor this year, Souvankham Thammavongsa, as she winnowed to those she most wished to include. *BCP* invites a different guest editor each year to take fresh stock of Canadian poetry in this way. As such, the anthology functions as a yearbook, an annual, rigorous, survey of the most accomplished new work by Canadian poets, always slightly skewed by a given editor's perspective.

The job of guest editing *BCP* is no light undertaking, and those who step up demonstrate a concern for our literature that extends beyond their own creative contributions. Their service here signifies a contribution of a different sort, to the conversation around what our poetry amounts to, what we make of it, and why. It behooves me here to draw attention to the private toil of all those poets—whether found within this anthology or not—who devotedly string words together, never knowing whether the string will hold. I note, too, the teams of journal editors who unravel vast wads of those strings to tease out glimmering strands; and the cheerful, overworked crew at Biblioasis who weave together all the many parts of this anthology. I lament the absence this year of my stalwart and brilliant former advisory editor, Luke Hathaway, who worked by my side for three joyful, productive years (at that time as Amanda Jernigan). I will so miss sharing with Luke the wonder of a poem's detangling before our eyes, revealing its inner gleam.

It happens that Zuroski's simple poem, which cradles a quiet ferocity and is composed chiefly of plain, functional words such as *what* and *have* and *we*, shares some affinity with Thammavongsa's own work. A formidable author and poet of spare, simple language herself, Thammavongsa has proudly spoken of the "ugly" little words on which she builds her verse, such as *this, is, it*: "There is nothing elegant or delicate about them. They are small and poor." (I discuss this in an essay I wrote on Thammavongsa's work for the *Walrus* in June 2019, where this quote also appears.) More recently, in fall 2020, amid a hubbub of literary acclaim—her moving, funny, and wrenching short-story collection, *How to Pronounce Knife*, won the Scotiabank Giller Prize while also drawing widespread international praise—Thammavongsa told the *Globe and Mail*, "I do savour the acknowledgment, and the fact that the writing that I do is seen. But also that the people I write about are seen and heard. Their experiences, our experiences, are at the centre of a story. But in a way that anybody could relate to."

To those who read or study or write poetry, especially in Canada, Thammavongsa was seen and heard long before her fiction made her a literary celebrity. The author of four remarkable poetry collections, the most recent of which is 2019's *Cluster*, she says, "My poems don't think *for* you, they think *with* you." She grants her readers the respect and autonomy she accords "The Black Ant," one of the many small creatures that move across the pages of her 2003 debut, *Small Arguments*. Treating its title as the start of a sentence, the poem begins:

> will go into
> > an unpaved city
>
>
> > > There will be no light
> > > > to lead its way,

                    no compass
                                to direct it
                                            only a digging to reach beyond,

Naturally, Thammavongsa's eye, her ear, her own most potent concerns as a reader, and as a writer, came into play as she narrowed her selection. Not all the poems she chose are as sparsely adorned as Zuroski's. I urge you, before you take in "a wing" and all that follows, to read Thammavongsa's frank and inviting introductory essay, in which she reveals something of her relationship with writing and poetry, as well as how she approached this anthology—work that, for a person who cares about words and language as Thammavongsa does, amounted to a sacred task.

I, meanwhile, shall keep my eye on the terror stowed, like that wing in a jar, in Zuroski's poem. It prepares us for the mood of unease—awareness of our fragility?—that ripples through this year's anthology. That fragility is balanced by an assertion of will, of basic being. It's the unflagging "digging to reach / beyond" of Thammavongsa's black ant, which ventures without light or compass into its "unpaved city."

It's tempting to read Covid and other 2020 turmoils into the tensions caught in these pages. However, many if not most of the pieces here would have been drafted before our first whiff of pandemic life. One exception is Maureen Hynes' "All clear," an early lockdown poem in which the months draw "silver & plastic & elastic songs / out of our tightened lungs." Another is Canisia Lubrin's "In the Middle of the Burning," in which "the forces who claim they love us / level our lives to crust." This breakneck, brutal response to the 2020 Black Lives Matter uprisings following George Floyd's death reaches into the deep, tragic history at the core of our contemporary crisis: "the centuries-wide dance / of swapped shackles for knees / their batons and miscellany." For me, the poem's most chilling moment occurs in one short line, alone on the page: "I dare not sing." Chilling; also triumphant. Also ominous. For the words do sound in our ears. What danger might the person face who sings despite them, with them, because of them?

You *will*, like the hand in Barbara Nickel's breathtaking ode and lament, "Essential Tremor," tremble as you read *BCP* this year. You'll hear, ironically loud and clear, Margaret Atwood's soft prayer "for a white shore." With Louise Carson you'll "watch and learn / how it is to live / the end of a life." You'll come to understand, with Randy Lundy, how "violence is like that—it works up close and at great distances like spookily conjoined subatomic particles."

Terror, like (obviously) poetry itself, predates Covid. It predates racism, slavery, and police brutality. It predates environmental devastation.

I give you David Ezra Wang's desperate quest for a place to be "in public, but unseen"; Kitty Cheung's sinister shot glass nudged "behind a jar of hoisin sauce"; the spirit of Judith Krause's mother in the basement, swinging on hangers.

I give you Dani Couture's roadside memorial: "A front door / to forever."

What we have here is a gathering of poems that, taken together, form a kind of proof to American poet Mary Ruefle's assertion in her essay "On Fear" that "perpetual fear is a propellant into the innocent, fearless and vulnerable world of the senses." In this—dare I say fearless—essay, Ruefle rehabilitates our oft-maligned feelings by outlining the scientifically defined difference between the instinctual *emotion* of fear—which "drives all animals away from life-threatening situations"—and *feelings* of fear, complex sensations that blend emotions with "memories, experience, and *intelligence*." (Ruefle's italics.) She calls fear "the great motivator," and, in a passage that offers a formidable answer to the perpetual question *Why poetry?*, writes: "As far back as I could remember, every minute of my life had been an emergency in which I was paralyzed with fear. Feelings of fear, being at least in part cognitive, and therefore thoughts, often constitute knowledge. For instance, the knowledge that one is going to die. This is a fear one can have while lying in a hammock on a beautiful day. And it can lead to an emergency of feeling that often results in a poem."

Fear thrums inside of poems because poets put it there in order to be able to size it up, contain it, and, however briefly, set it aside in order to live. From the "familiar steps we cling to" in Unnati Desai's "an ode to my brother's forehead stitches" to the repetition in Kate Cayley's "Attention" of "folding along the crease / until the crease finds itself"; from the "feathers on the kitchen floor" in Eve Joseph's harrowing "family history" to "this rallied congregation, / with its leaky canopy of perfume" in Sue Sinclair's "The Peonies"; we see, we touch, we hear, we smell. In these bursts of scent and sight, texture and sound, fear isn't conquered; it dissolves in a jumble of sensations. It becomes a mere irritation or distraction, nudged aside by the feel of a cool sheet between the fingers, the heady scent of riotously blooming peonies. The bewitching twitch of a feather lures the eye from the crisis.

In Kayla Czaga's "The Peace Lily," the narrator struggles to keep a grocery-store plant alive. In this poem, we sidestep fear—that fear of death that may strike anywhere, anytime: in Ruefle's sun-soaked hammock, say, or as we regard a pot of hideous, wilting leaves.

> Like a famous connoisseur
> of death, it took its time:
> every last leaf withered
> into a black ash that stuck
> on the shelf, and what
> remained in the pot
> resembled the dregs
> of a great forest fire.

How does Czaga turn us, laughing, toward death? Consider that "empty gulf" John Steffler finds concealed behind statements in "What Kind of Tracks Are These?", a poem that, in being composed entirely of questions, manages to be both funny and terrifyingly pertinent in an age when polarities and the certainties that feed them thrive. In her strange and beautiful poem, "Civilization lives in the throat," Beth Goobie reminds us that "not knowing is the beginning of everything." Then she sends us out into the city, where:

> The street itself is a throat, each of us carried in its pulse—
> city landscaped by voice. Civilization lives in the cry
> that lifts like early morning light up skyscraper windows

And suppose you allow yourself to stop and hear that cry— even if it be a cry of anguish? You pause with tilted head, listening, as this cry rises with the morning light. "One shared note," Goobie writes, "can listen you into a strange city / where people you've never met smile like songs you want to learn".

Way back in 1941, in the midst of another global crisis, the Second World War, literary theorist Kenneth Burke published his book *The Philosophy of Literary Form*, which became a seminal twentieth-century text. In it, he proposes that humans make poetry to comfort themselves. Poetry serves, he writes, as "a ritualistic way of arming us to confront perplexities and risks. It would protect us." Eighty years on, the idea that poetry might protect us—not *from* life's perplexities and risks, but from existential injury or failure of courage as we *confront* life's difficulties, rather like a suit of armour hammered out of words—remains startling and magnificent. Burke's theory on *how* these poems go about protecting us is striking. He likens the sleight-of-hand creative labour poets employ to Perseus grasping that he can regard Medusa's reflection and survive: that he can face, at safe remove, the monster who would turn him to stone at the merest *direct* glance. Burke writes (using the pronoun "he" as per his times), "The poet's style, his form (a social idiom), is this mirror, enabling him to confront the risk, but by the protection of an indirect reflection."

7

The wonder, for readers, is to encounter, in the form of a poem, that "indirect reflection" of fear: the palpable fear of a fellow being, caught, say, on the wing of a moth. From her title onward, Zuroski lands our gaze, and thus our minds, on that tragedy, that treasure, that wing. Picturing it, I'm reminded of Ruefle's contention that fear steers us toward the senses. This relates to how the philosopher Gaston Bachelard holds the image above metaphor. In *Poetics of Space* he writes that "images are incapable of repose. Poetic revery . . . never falls asleep. Starting with the simplest of images, it must always set the waves of the imagination radiating."

The wing was lost, severed from its original purpose. It's become, instead, by way of a poem, a remnant and proof. A sight upon which to rest our eyes, as it lights up our minds.

The launched imagination rocks us upon its waves.

Anita Lahey
Ottawa / unceded Algonquin, Anishinabek territory
April 2021

INTRODUCTION

I grew up in a home without books. My parents didn't go to school and they did not read for pleasure. They worked long hours in jobs nobody wanted. Any time I saw a bookshelf at a public library or at school or at my friend's house, I would beg my parents to take a photograph of me in front of it— the way people do when they go on vacation and think they might not ever get to see all that again. I always wanted to be a writer. It didn't matter that I didn't know how to become one. It didn't matter what that might take. I just wrote. In high school, I ran the poetry club. No one came to my meetings even though I announced them in the morning along with the sports and club meets. Every week, I showed up and held those meetings anyway. Sometimes someone would drop by, stick their head into the room, and say, "What's happening here?" I would tell them it was the poetry club and be met with great pity, and then I would be left alone. My high school yearbook photograph would tell a different story, as photographs often do. The photograph there shows a poetry club of more than one member. The yearbook photographer asked a few students walking by in the hallway if they would come and pretend to be in the club. I bring this memory up because in editing this anthology I see that I am not alone as I was, and everyone here isn't pretending. They are real. I found writing here that taught me to always find something interesting, always find something to be excited about, even if there is no one there to cheer you on. Many years ago, just like the poets in these literary magazines and journals, I sent my poems out in an envelope with a self-addressed, stamped envelope inside. The poems arrived somewhere and sat around for many months or a year or years. Sometimes they didn't arrive at all, and there was no way to know. No one spoke for them. I would get replies about regrets, a line or two about the next time, to try again. I don't know how many rejection letters I got. There were so many. After a while, they don't even register. The number of acceptance letters, I do know. That number is manageable. I remember too the feeling of seeing myself in print. My name like a birth certificate telling of some true fact. Last year, I read Canadian poets published in magazines and journals that published poetry in print or online or in a newsletter subscription. I read Canadian poets wherever they appeared around the world. Sometimes someone would post about where they were published on social media, and I would seek out their poem. A friend told me about a poem written by a student of theirs, and I went to read that too. I overheard conversations and made notes. The voices I was drawn to were the ones that got in and got out quickly, that said unusual things, that were clear, spare, and plain, that made me laugh out loud. I noticed the voices that barely ever survive to make it on to the page. The ones whose use of sound and language and repetition and rhythms get edited out. I held onto those voices to bring them here. I didn't pay attention to the name of the writer, how many books they'd published, what prizes they'd won. It's possible to be no one, to have no book, to make work that is meaningful and valuable and beautiful without a crown or someone else's say-so. I looked only at the poem and what it did. The word after the word. Some I knew right away to put in the anthology. With others, it took a few months—I felt haunted by a poem and couldn't forget what was done and said and managed. What I found was the work volunteers, editors, those who work at literary magazines, discovered first. It is their work, their discovery. These were the possibilities they created for writers to make it on to the page. I just held on to them. So many of us get to see our first poems in a magazine before we see our names on the spines of our own books. I understand that the poems I selected may not be considered the best by someone else, or even by the poets themselves. I don't care. I will hold my love for your poem and wait for you to join me someday, though it is possible you won't ever come to love it simply because it's yours. This book is about what I saw and read and loved, and want you to see and read and love. I understand, too, the writers who hoped to see themselves in this anthology but are not here. I have been where your hope is, and I can tell you: keep going. The best Canadian poetry is probably not in these pages, because the poet didn't send it out to a magazine, or didn't have time to sit down to write it—because of life. Life takes up time, whole days. Sometimes you have to count bags and bags of cash five levels below the ground for a big bank because it's a job that will get you to the next minute, the next hour, the next year. How to find that poet? To the editors who are looking and reading: I hope, in the years to come, that you will find that poet, the one life happened to this year. I know the literary magazines and journals are standing by. And to those who are waiting for confidence and courage and advice. There is no such thing as confidence. A poet doesn't need courage. You can be scared and write with that fear. And advice? Well, stop asking for someone else's advice. Who's to say you don't already know what is brilliant and spectacular.

Souvankham Thammavongsa
Toronto
April 2021

a wing on the pavement, now kept in a jar

Eugenia Zuroski

how much money do we have

we have negative money

what does that mean

we have less than zero money

so we are poor

no, we are fine. we are better than fine. we are fortunate

but how

yes, but how

and what do moths eat

yes, what

— from *Room*

acne, blood, and all things that flow

David Ezra Wang

just today I reminded my parents that I only have two more
months of being a teenager. in further conversation, my dad,
who argued that nineteen years olds are not teenagers, told
me he's reminiscent of the time when I was still a child

today I stayed at home because there's a huge red pimple
growing on my nose, alongside the fifty plus scars and other
deformations on my face.

I went to the rooftop of my apartment building.
that's the only place I can be in public, but unseen
in known, but in hiding

today I thought about a cool art project
I'll cover my body with a big piece of white cloth
become architectural sculpture or something
worth your time, something worth a gallery,
something worth a show, something, of worth

today I read the Bible
and today I washed my face, twice
today I prayed to God about my skin

on the rooftop I played my music
I whispered into the air and wondered
if anyone would fall in love with me if I really exfoliated my face
like really
like
rubbed my face against fragments of stone in salt water
scrubbed till my hands join the tides of the ocean
scrubbed till there was nothing left but blood and all things that flow

but right now I'm going to bed
I'm going to think about some good things.
the right words haven't come to me yet
I'll ask my dad, I'll ask my mom, I'll ask God.
tomorrow morning I will wake up a day closer to my
    twentieth birthday
and I'll get back to you then

I don't know why I look like this,
do you? tell me tomorrow

— from *Ricepaper Magazine*

All clear

Maureen Hynes

It comes out in March, by the back fence
   — Lorine Niedecker, "Progression"

March, yes, & April & May & even all
those months before, say, back to November—
each drew silver & plastic & elastic songs
out of our tightened lungs. The sewing machine
had been repaired, the masks colourful & haphazard.
Finally, May Day, the doctor called with questions
about poetry & emptiness. His shyness
both infected & cured me. It turned into
something stone-hard that I could lob
from the city's highest bridge clear into
the unvaccinated river. But no, but no,
that's unkind—the doctor was considerate
& knew exactly where my fear was sitting.
Front row centre.

— from *Arc Poetry Magazine*

an ode to my brother's forehead stitches
Unnati Desai

you were born from the single stair/that lay connecting
two fractured homes/you introduced yourself through the
streaming blood/giving start to the first cry of the night/
some may call you a stain/a blemish/a scar/but you/you are a
thread/weaving together pieces of our childhood/connecting
us to each other/you/are a storyteller/repeating the tale of the
night in my grandmother's/arms/my mother's white dupatta
red/the cold darkness taking over/screams demanding silence
so we can hear him run inside/and then/a smiling face/with
you/a reminder/of how easy it is to slip away/to tear off into
the world/but in the drowning darkness/it's the familiar steps
we cling to.

— from *Room*

Another Woman in Canada

George K Ilsley

A collection of one star reviews of Dear Life *by Alice Munro*

10) Alice Munro may have won the Nobel Prize, but has not mastered the art of the short story.

9) A seemingly endless and pointless journey to nowhere. With no reward.

8) It's as if this author thinks she can write about ordinary people and make us care. Why should I care about a shop girl who loses her job?

7) Nothing happens. People have affairs, start new jobs, siblings die. There was no point to any of it.

6) So tedious not even worth talking about. Waste of time. Not worth reading.

5) Every time I pick up Alice Munro I think, great, a whole new story about a woman in Canada.

4) It all boils down to this: You can't love a book just because you feel guilty for not loving it.

3) Never even heard of this author until she won the Pulitzer. Needless to say, will not bother reading anything else by this extremely dull and uninspired writer.

2) The characters are boring and bland, like Canadians. Might be of interest to someone who wants to read about life long ago in a small town on the Plains of Canada.

1) Ambiguity really has no place in a compilation entitled "Dear Life."

— from *Geist*

Asch's Line Study in the Current Anthropocene

Paola Ferrante

At the end of the world we saw the lines; the answers were
so obvious. Sometimes we chose b, when the answer was c;
we knew the answer was c, but everyone said b. With b there
was the line that smiled, circled the inside of a hug, cut the
sun in half on a lake so we could remind each other, in slow
morning softness over coffee, that at least there was still sun
today. With b, the line divided two-lane road trip highways
between going back and forward, and sometimes there was
caution. We could see the line was yellow, but faded yellow,
and sometimes yellow was suggestion same way we'd never
see our hands were red from disappearing ladybugs, the ones
that weren't collecting on our windshields. When the line
was b, we kept driving; no one stopped for red. With b, the
line was chalk, children's drawings of a home on driveways,
those little branches on a family tree, or the smile on the
mouth of a boy with the tilt of your own childhood, going
down even the reddest of slides just one more time. We didn't
choose c; we said that no one would. We didn't choose c, as
though our children's children would still have woods to
wander in, see what's lovely in their dark and deep. When
the line was shadow, dark and deep beneath our beds, we
smelled the bedroom smell of one we loved and shut our eyes
to everything not underneath the covers. We said we didn't
see it move, that line, the colour of a river, and fast as a river
too. The line that moved became the water, what used to be
a beach but ended, then wildfire cutting where the trees had
ended, until the do not cut last spruce was cut a year ago.
Of course we crossed that line; of course, we wouldn't see it.
Before the river in the sky became a mudslide, we stood for
elevator talk about the weather as though we'd never tried to
buy the rain, as though the rain was not canaries, slamming
into windows. We chose, but stood in grocery lines and talked

of whether, as though we could still choose a time to see, as though we'd get to choose when the power would go out.

— from *Grain*

Attention

Kate Cayley

And if attention is repetition, folding along the crease
until the crease finds itself, the act of making
hollowing out the same groove, as in marriage
studying, over years, the same face, the same
permeable body, as in children, their fury, their
fraught going-forward, thinning out your life
like a membrane that will not break, their lives
a repetition that alters in the telling, your attention
is for them, and theirs outstripping you
and stripping you of anything they find useful, yet
carrying you with them, a husk pinned to the inside
pocket of their lives, as in repeating
the action of rising at dawn, as the poet
who wrote on the back of recipe cards attended
sternly to the rising bread, attended each
repeated blade of grass on the same Amherst lawn
for as long as her days repeated themselves, each day
compressed itself into the other, then I will
believe that language was sung first, before speech,
that language was song, praise
that could not be contained, for the world
that repeated, that, each day, continued.

— from *Grain*

bikini tits shot glass

Kitty Cheung

when my mom married my stepdad
signed a deal along with his sponsorship papers
he brought into our house
a local souvenir

a shot glass
moulded into the shape of a woman's bust
nipples erect and all
red and white bikini
little maple leafs
painted onto see-through breasts

he keeps it on the dining table
so I stare over my bowl of
cereal, fried rice, plain rice
pointed glass nipples
breasts plump, indulgent
hard, cold

before my mom married my stepdad
our home was full of women
mom, sister, me

mom thinks the shot glass is funny
a little joke
no matter how much my sister and I protest
try to explain our Western ideas
to this inherently Eastern woman

how do you say "objectification" in Cantonese?
how do you explain misogyny to the most important woman
    in your life?

how do you criticize the patriarchy when it's all she's ever
    known?
so ingrained in tradition
disbelief that she would stay on the side
where she and her daughters would lose the most

sometimes, as I pause to carefully separate
the fish bones from the flesh in my mouth
I hide the shot glass
nudge it behind a jar of hoisin sauce
a bunch of bananas

but it always emerges
this prized possession
with its demeaning glint
as if one of the bone shards has caught in my throat
refusing to go away
no matter how much I squirm and cough

— from *Ricepaper Magazine*

Civilization lives in the throat

Beth Goobie

like a bird cross-stitching a backyard with sound.
The throat is the hollow stem of a wine glass,
the root of the question mark that rises out of the heart
into the head. The throat connects heartbeat and word;
can you tell by its rhythm which speech drinks its truths
and which does not thirst. The lark ascends in your communications
or it does not. A child sits on a bank, piping a river
through a wooden flute. Listening at a window
a woman hums sun's delight across water
as she sketches architectural plans for a new city hall.
People flow through those glass doors, reflections approach
like ideas surfacing, words seeking air. The inner
leaps toward the outer like the pulse in the throat
shared by everyone you pass on a downtown street.
The street itself is a throat, each of us carried in its pulse—
city landscaped by voice. Civilization lives in the cry
that lifts like early morning light up skyscraper windows
above the slumped panhandler, his cap a silent mouth.
Well-wishers drop coins and hurry their own surrender away.
What is language if we do not speak what stammers the tongue?
Not knowing is the beginning of everything.
The same notes play us all, though we arrange into different chords;
one shared note can listen you into a strange city
where people you've never met smile like songs you want to learn
and we're all busking our heartbeats for a dime.
There perched on a street corner bench, a lark embroiders
our sidewalk anthem. It ascends.

— from *Prairie Fire*

Dawson

Emily Pohl-Weary

Here, I am restless under sunsets that endure
all night. Skin smeared orange, pink, yellow and blue

I thought I'd be alone up north
instead, there's too much sky
black spruce, sticky poplar, trembling aspen, white birch
gold flakes, grey ashes, purple flowers, pink rock, fireweed

The city had become
a fork in the eye
a boot to the neck
a parrot squawking

Here, I linger thirsty
at the confluence between a muddy river and a clear one
sucking in a thick stream of wildfire smoke
watching the glaciers release silt

Perpetual sun has taught me
to draw the blinds, swim in clouds, dance again, be kind

— from *Taddle Creek*

Day of the Dead

Judith Krause

The day after Halloween
it takes me less than an hour

to pack up the decorations
I had chosen with such care

in the weeks prior—
golden spiders

with hairy legs
and fearsome fangs,

glow-in-the-dark
skulls with toothless

grins sticking out of
garden pots,

and ghosts with hollow
eyes and cheeks

fluttering from eaves.
Gone now till next year

this mix of sinister
and silly, welcome

signs to those who dare
knock on my door for

a treat of cheap chocolate
or candy. Not much left

in this part of the world
to remind us the evening

has less to do with
the living than the dead.

I sigh, hurry everything
to the basement to

store next to the spot where
my mother's things

are boxed, one unmarked
carton stacked on top

of another, a tower
that leans like a cracked

sarcophagus. Under a ceiling
vent, her favourite sweaters,

ones I took home to wash
the week before she died,

hang from the bars of an old
wooden laundry rack.

Each time the heat kicks in,
they swing back to life.

— from *Grain*

Driver's Ed at 41

Dani Couture

Between dated video re-enactments more current
to memory than historical, the instructor relays the story
of a woman he knew who'd left her garage door open,
her pick-up's windows rolled down. On backing out
onto the gravel drive, she saw a bat flattened
against her visor. Punched it, killed it, bagged it,
and put it in the freezer before taking it to the vet
for testing. *What should you do? Look in the direction
you want to go. Roll down the windows. Signal
and pull over to the shoulder. Deal with it.* I look back—
to the first person who told me at fifteen that my friend,
newly sixteen, had died. T-boned by a truck on the 20
one late fall morning. To the teacher, who, when I asked
to leave didn't say, *Sorry*—only, *Funny, I never saw you
two together,* as if she ever saw us. Every holiday,
the roadside memorial miraculously redecorated. A front door
to forever. It's already been years since it's been years
that she's been dead longer than she was alive.
Each visit home, I get older. I pass by birthday balloons
caught in crosswinds, Christmas wreaths, pastel
Easter eggs, in the passenger seat of anyone who
will ferry me past the past. Both coming and going, I lift
a hand behind the safety glass and say, "Hi, Mary."
In a basement classroom, under the glare of shuddering
fluorescents, I turn to the teen beside me, ask if
it's too late to start again or if I should just keep going.

— from *The Malahat Review*

Essential Tremor

Barbara Nickel

If only it were that: a little
trembling in the hand. If we could tell
your leg be still and still it would. Be it-
self before we heard the news, reeling,
before the shift and the settle into restless
in bed, the shudder as you roll—
here and gone and here momentous
as aurora and nothing I can hold.
Ends always with me spoon-feeding
and push-chairing, the secret life
of drool which maybe isn't half so bad as it looms;
in our room would gather the minuscule
beauties, for instance wind setting off the aspen,
every quaver in your lovely hand.

— from *The Walrus*

family history

Eve Joseph

I am experiencing bouts of amnesia. Caught in the mesmerizing contradictions of time. One minute goes by and the whole story gets rewritten whereas years pass and the hands on the clock barely move. My grandfather took his younger brother under the table and started to cut his throat with the blunt edge of a knife. His mother had a fit and brought him a chicken. "Kill this instead," she said, holding a glass of brandy for him in case he fainted. Forgetfulness is different than not remembering. Were it not for the feathers on the kitchen floor I wouldn't believe a word of it.

— from *The Malahat Review*

Flatline

Margaret Atwood

Things wear out. Also fingers.
Gnarling sets in.
Your hands crouch in their mittens.
Forget chopsticks, and buttons.

Feet have their own agendas.
They scorn your taste in shoes
and ignore your trails, your maps.

Ears are superfluous:
What are they for,
those alien pink flaps?
Skull fungus.

The body, once your accomplice,
is now your trap.
The sunrise makes you wince:
too bright, too flamingo.

After a lifetime of tangling,
of knotted snares and lacework,
of purple headspace tornados
with their heartrace and rubble,
you crave the end of mazes

and pray for a white shore,
an ocean with its horizon;
not, so much, bliss
but a flat line you steer for.

No more hiss and slosh,
no reefs, no deeps,
no throat rattle of gravel.

It sounds like this:

— from *The New Yorker*

From the Nurse's Cabin Porch, Keats Island

Hayden Ward

Mum cuts off the heads
of the hornets. The boy's hair
is curly and blond

from the sun, inside
the hornets are caught, biting
and stinging. The boy

is crying and Mum
holds both his hands in her one
while her other hand

decapitates them.
The furious and frightened
hornets stop writhing

and she begins to
untangle their little arms
and bodies. She cuts

out some of his hair.
Holding them like marionettes,
she is offering

them to the crying
boy. Wrapped up in his hair, he
buries them under

the nurse's cabin
porch where there could be spiders
and I found a bird

wing all maggoty
once, rotting, its body gone.
Mum is kneeling down

now beside the boy,
balanced on the balls of her
feet. Are they praying?

— from *Grain*

Gravel

Arielle Twist

I asked the creator to make me soft
told them I was trying to prove that I
was worthy of a love that was forgiving,
a love worth losing, while losing myself.
I begged the sky to bring him back to me
this man with brown eyes and a wide smile
but all they gave me was rain, as he roamed
the streets, concrete and sea consuming us
both here. And still, I am finding gravel behind
my eyes, coughing up oceans like my body is
trying to make an island for us to exist again,
or maybe for us to exist for the first time.

— from *The Fiddlehead*

Grip to Ground Connector

Ken Babstock

Geometry of the indolent, the shirkers,
      the holstered ratchet and Metallica T,
the rigger in cycling gloves, the paid-up member,
      the daily, the skinhead reading García
Márquez, the hungover biochemist hoarding
      three treatments at mom's, the paroled,
the stargazer, the undercover cop, the capoeira
      brown belt who went down on Jolie,
C-clamp jockeys, the naphthalene moon-wranglers,
      the diabetic gamers, the art historians,
the redeployed craft services chef, the butch
      lesbian boxers, the acned, the hyper,
the wrong-channel merchant, the father of four,
      the speed-dealing Rhodes Scholar,
fantasy novelists chewing holes in their cheeks,
      colorists, arborists, entomologists,
the Benedictine novice quoting Jay-Z
      over lunch, the orphaned and over-sexed,
Trotskyists glaring at cherry tomatoes,
      epileptics, onanists, some dude with a recipe
for killer grilled cheese, bipeds, bisexuals,
      brown baggers, gymnasts, monarchists,
pedophiles, and originalists. We all just sat there—
      one, two stacked, one flat one upended,
three if in truck after wrap—while the films of our
      deaths got made under budget.

— from *Poetry*

I Really Liked Your Reading Last Night

Elana Wolff

You came alone and sat at the back of the room.

We gave each other a friendly hug
and chatted before the show. Your breath smelled

thinly of gin. "There are a lot of good poets,"
you said and smiled, by way of slant reply,

after I'd commended your performance.
It's slant like that

that makes one
feel disclosed.

You didn't introduce your poems,
just read them in a modulated tone—

"I" embedded,
hunkered down: a foreign correspondent in a war zone.

I wanted a book, you didn't have one to sell.
We both had salvation in pieces we read.

I couched it
Salvia divinorum, as in the psychoactive plant.

You used the word straight-up—like you had earned it.

— from *Taddle Creek*

i tell my mother everything

Tina Do

which is to say: I only tell her about the things that are safe—
yes mom, I got an A in English,

no mom, I don't look at boys, only textbooks
of course, the haircut you gave me in front of the bathroom
    sink is fine

I *understand*—I won't go to the sleepover
yes, it's ok to sell the piano so we can pay rent—

mom, let me explain the movie—
this character lives, this one dies, this is how everything ends.

or rather, this is how it begins:
hey mom, I got a C+ in math to the surprise of my peers

and loved a boy whose name was the same as a crowbar
until he laughed in my face and called me ugly

I wish we hadn't sold the piano—
the one I cherished with all my fingers until I was 16

with a crack   in the middle C key because I dropped
the metronome on it trying to cheat the kitchen timer

you set for two hours—but I was never going to be a concert
    pianist
at least not the one you rented out to aunts and uncles

who were never mine except in ways that didn't matter
paid in nothing but gummy smiles, sore cheeks,

no boundaries and *thêm mát bài hát con—*
I have never held a cigarette, but I want to know what it's like

to be a proper rebel—leather jacket, army boots, fishnets, and
    piercings,
hold smoke in my lungs like I have something to prove.

I shoplifted as a teenager
because you couldn't afford to buy yourself new underwear

and pay for our groceries, so I stuffed panties
into my coat sleeves and put them in your drawer.

I guess I am saying I don't know how
to live like I've been loved my entire life

that I only watch movies in short bursts
pause   after   every   twenty-minute   interval

pause   *yes,* I'll take you to the store / the doctor / the dentist /
    the post office
pause   *knives* is spelt with *k* / oh, it means the same as *dao*

rewind *mom,* this is the story that *bà nôi* told me about you:
a girl brings up four brothers for a mother that is there but *not really*

leaves one continent for another to settle in uncertainty
sews tapestries for a history that has chosen to write—her out—

about the men who thought warfare was between a woman's legs,
then went home to their wives and loved their families—

all this to say: my mother doesn't tell me about the dangerous things,
that she ran with knives before she could spell them in English

cut her hand on blades before she knew how to say *blood*,
tries to cook *bún bò huê* with a half-formed tongue

which is to say: this is how we live. this is how we die.
this is how everything ends—*lingchi*

— from *The / temz / Review*

In the Middle of the Burning

Canisia Lubrin

notice now pictures of awful things on top our head
the freight that barricades this view, how enough
how the law batter down the dogged tide we make
the world shoring its dark scars between seasons
as though to hold it together only by a flame
is here a voice to please enough the blunt
borderlessness of this grief turning our heads to rubble
the lunacy of nothing so limning as death in the streets
in these vibrating hours where the corners talk back
need I simply run my tongue along the granite sky and live

to know how lost the millionth life somewhere today
the swift shape of roads new names combust, the sum
of anthems flooding the world with the eye's sudden and narrow
saltwater and streets ziplined with screams at the pitch of
    cooking pots
then tear gas, then pepper spray, then militarized lies unzipping
body bags, oh, our many many there, our alive and just born,
and that is how to say let's fuck it up, we the beat and we the loud
tuning forks and the help arriving empty-handed
propping the hot news of new times on our head

days like these pleat whatever the hollow year must offer
between the not-yet-dead and those just waking up
it will not be the vanished thing that we remember
it will be what we exchanged close to midnight
like smugglers high-wiring the city, hoarding the thoughts
of ours we interrupted midway to discovering the velocity
of the burning world below
of our language in the lateness of our stuck and reckless love

where the forces who claim they love us
level our lives to crust—the centuries-wide dance
of swapped shackles for knees
their batons and miscellany
thrown at our whole lives demanding our mothers
raise from their separate rooms, separate graves, today
to save who and me? I open the book to a naked page
where nothing clatter my heart, what head
what teeth cling to broadside, roll alias after
alias with a pen at their dull tribunes and shrines
imagine our heirlooms of shot nerves make a life
given to placards and synergies and elegies, but more

       last things: where letters here where snow in May
     where the millennium unstitches the quartered earth
             in June, how many today to the viral fire
               the frosted rich and their forts, but not
           the fulsome rage of my people unpeaced
             mute boots with somber looks appear
   a fearsome autumn ending spring, though we still hear

I dare not sing

another song to dig a hole this time for the lineages
of magnolias where the offspring bring a hand to cover
our mouth, our heaping lives, who sit who burn who drop
three feet to the tar, who eat and demolish the thing
that takes our head, the thing that is no more
the place that never was except a burning learned

just once and not again when the darker working's race

— from *Poem-a-Day*

Is it Safe?

Ronna Bloom

Tell us, they said, no one died
or killed or took their life
and left it in the basement.
Tell us there are no people ghosts or creature ghosts.
Tell us what colour is a good colour and will it be safe?
Will a condo rise above? Or a sinkhole below?
Please tell us, they said, if you will leave the light on
when you go, if you'll come back,
and what you did here and with whom,
and will we be lovely and will we be lonely
and will we be lucky,
how much will it cost, they said, and how loud,
for how long, they cried, for how long?

— from *Literary Review of Canada*

Knots

Courtney Bates-Hardy

What would it feel like
to write all of the knots
from my shoulders? To trace
my pen from stem
to sternum, to slip the nib
into my skin and pare down
to the poem? If I could
peel my skull like an apple
to the core, could I make
parchment from my flesh?

I would crack open the occipital
bone for the pink of it, suck
the meat from the bones,
lie satisfied and spent and
open like an egg. Instead,
the metaphor is lost. I poke
each knot with my pen.
The ink dies on my skin, and the knots
have tied up my fingers.

— from *Poetry Pause*

Learning to Die

Jan Zwicky

My father in my dream trying
to teach me. We're joking and talking
—such good times! Even better
than of old. How relaxed he is, how happy
we're together. And I think perhaps
I start to understand, the joy
of the dark night, my dead father
laughing, a bell somewhere
steady through snow, and time
slowing, or is it my heart at last
hearing its name, and now I am running
to meet it, I am running, running.

— from *Prairie Fire*

Loss +

Zoe Imani Sharpe

As far as accounting goes it goes Cornflakes. It goes
    cucumbers and cigarettes.
It goes *count the women concerned with counting*: Coleman,
    Beatty, Niedecker,
Lorine's neat but never nice haiku. Five and seven. Weighted
    silver. Affixed.

Some man stamps my chequebook while economy presses
    my linear dress.
Wave and wave and man. Sleep to count sheep. All this talk of
    Patek Philippe—
thirty thou' to a hundred thou' 'nother hundred thou'.... Static
    is counting

on me to be countable. Lose that oscillating digit. A country's
    objects smoothed
and folded over the wet heart, squinting. My fingers,
    an abacus of light.
What do we expect of lineage but to amount? I get this Desire
    on discount.

— from *The Puritan*

Love you

Louise Carson

For my daughter

You watch and learn
   how it is to live
      the end of a life.

I eat a few favourite foods,
   drink and smoke
      if I want to.

I don't waste my time
   with people who don't love me.
      Love me.

— from *Poetry Pause*

Mango

Ian Keteku

When the sadness softens
and the sky is clear
I will carry my father by feather or feet
to the ridge where he was born
where his mother still drinks
from the fall.

He will sit
until the swelling softens
he relives his life—a young mango
growing into grey

too frail to feed anything
but the ground with its body.

— from *Arc Poetry Magazine*

Memory of the Black Lake

David Ly

I remember it clearly because it was cloudy
the night after a choir of mermaids spawned.

The surface sparkled with their bioluminescent egg sacs
like a sheet of glass reflecting a night sky

speckled with blue and yellow stars.
You sat across from me in the rowboat, dipping the oars

breaking the still water. I tightened my hand
on your knee reminding you to be

mindful of the fragile heartbeats.
But you already understood to gingerly guide us

so nothing would be in danger as we crossed
the black lake in silence.

— from *Arc Poetry Magazine*

Morning Pages

Randy Lundy

Rain late last evening, near the end of April, and a light freeze
overnight. This morning the windows feathered with frost as
if the world had left fingerprints detailing its dreams of flight,
and out for a cigarette with your first coffee, two dogs, and
evaporate rising in the backyard, like smoke from a bush fire,
up in the Pasqua hills, among the trees, just north and east of
the peat bog where your cousin Elmer works, and where he
sets up trail cams to catch ghost-like images of the caribou
whose tracks he's seen, where they come to calve in spring,
the tangled undergrowth and the soft, wet land protection
from the local wolf pack. And you are reading an article about
two young, female poets—one from Greenland and one from
the Marshall Islands—lives destroyed by the melting ice and
others by the steadily rising tides. Communities thousands of
miles apart. But violence is like that—it works up close and at
great distances like spookily conjoined subatomic particles.
For some reason, you think of a colleague at work, her saying,
I love Indigenous cultures. They're so beautiful, and you want
to tell her to just keep it to herself, that you don't give a
fuck, that the people don't need the wihtikow hunger of her
appreciation and praise. *Save it for your god,* you want to say.
You witnessed what she did with the old woman's teachings
about sage: she and her small, like-minded gang ran to the
nearest bush, threw down some tobacco, and stripped it bare,
then sat in the shade of a pickup truck and gossiped—they
huddled and clucked—while plucking the leaves from thin
branches. And you realise that image is an insult to chickens
everywhere, but at least you've still got your sense of humour,
even though you are feeling bitter this morning, like the taste
on your fingers after lighting a smudge, even though you do
nothing but sit down to play around with words, while the

controlled spin of the world whisks all of us into a future
devoid of human care and concern, or the lack thereof.

— from *Prairie Fire*

On Artificially Conceiving our Children

Pamela Mosher

We may have different thoughts
about what it means for a thing to be natural.

       I can't imagine anything more *real*
than stretching out   on an exam table
each month, listening to a gloved nurse expostulate
on the merits of relaxation while she inserts a unit
of recently thawed sperm into my uterus.

And at least for now, these
artificially conceived children are genuinely
indifferent to our process
of becoming their mothers.

They romp around the living room, dragging
blankets across the coffee table and rolling
through piles of pillows,
       their faces unguarded, laughter blooming
within the fragile walls of their small bodies.

    —from *Grain*

The Peace Lily

Kayla Czaga

The peace lily I bought
at Thrifty Foods for $4.99
taught me something
about beauty. When I saw
its poker-green leaves
and flowers, like studded
Jacobsen Egg Chairs,
I rushed it into my cart,
wheeled to the till, carried
it home, and centred it
atop a sunny bookshelf.
Within a week, its leaves
had black spots. A second
week saw its flowers gone.
My mother-in-law said
it needed repotting
and took it—returned it
in a larger pot, trimmed
of rot. Still, it withered.
The internet told me to
shield it from breezes,
to mist it, fertilize it,
and comb for mites. I did
everything, and in return,
it sent out one new flower,
alive as a child's hand,
which drooped before
ever really blooming.
To say the peace lily died
would be an understatement.
Like a famous connoisseur
of death, it took its time:

every last leaf withered
into a black ash that stuck
on the shelf, and what
remained in the pot
resembled the dregs
of a great forest fire.
I am not someone
who if you smashed all
her mirrors or splattered
her canvases with tar
would suffer very much,
but I admired the lily
and wanted it to thrive.
Yet the more I did for it
the less interested
it seemed in living,
and in the end—tipping it
out into my compost bin—
a bit of me loved
being done with it.

— from *The Walrus*

The Peonies

Sue Sinclair

They elbow their collective way past beauty—so essentially
plentiful, bullishly iterative, they encroach on the grotesque,
though beauty could be said to predict, even invite such a
     movement,
always at least a little too much of a good thing. Drenched with
     affect,
soaked through with a materiality that refuses to be marginalized,
this willful self-occupation, this rallied congregation,
with its leaky canopy of perfume, has no control over the assembly
and demands none, allows the sensorium to be pushed to its
     n^{th} degree,
sees exaggeration not as denial of reality but a way of displaying
one's commitment to it: the crowd has no permits and is loath
     to disperse.

— from *Grain*

Re: That One Part of My Brain That Will Never Leave Me Alone

Ottavia Paluch

A doesn't want to lift the fog so I can see the whole mess
    more clearly.
A makes people wonder why I won't look them in the eyes.
A threw eye contact out the window, that's why.
A thinks I can't ask questions—once, this was true.
A has stolen most of the answers.
A watches my meltdowns from afar.
A never offers to help.
A never taught me how to lie.
A never knew I was learning on my own.
A is made of dead stars I assume are still shining.

— from *Room*

Reckoning

Nina Philomena Honorat

There will be a reckoning.
A door swung open from
which a thousand moths will flutter.
Silence sharpened in depth—
word of mouth,   exhausted.
Flock of fallen angels
rummaging through
paper thin omens for the next apocalypse.
Howl-hurled prayer,
mocking-bird-song.

— from *Juniper*

Retirement Plans

Sarah Yi-Mei Tsiang

The phone rings all night
even though we've disconnected it.
Some things don't know
they're obsolete.
I wonder if I will be this way,
padding through corridors
in slippered feet, my voice
ringing and ringing
with no one to pick up.

— from *The Malahat Review*

Riddle

Mary Dean Lee

We were five, then four, then three

ribs twigs snapped

                                   tubes to breathe and eat

                 young saplings spinning out

he's there but not—

one broken
one swings wildly
one trembles

                             father rows to his island

                                    mother fills the jug

— from *Grain*

Seagulls

Matthew Rooney

Outcrop crags pierce sunken clouds.
Distant, grey seagulls singing
Circles—survey the soft shroud
To crown their rocky sovereign.

       Hurrah
            hurrah.

— from *Newfoundland Quarterly*

Self-Portrait with an Internal Conflict

Phoebe Wang

As if she were making an argument, not for beauty,
but for yellow tulips supple with purpose,
the patternless patina of a brass kettle, while the hand
that arranged them is suggested in the gathering,
the maturing, the waiting, the pause
of dusky blueberries, apples turned towards
the light, or away from it, the source of which is unseen.
And yet, beauty persists, because of what has been
removed so that each bundle of straw, each arrangement
could become the essence of itself, without rot or browning
or stains or the sticky bits of scraped-off tape and insects,
and that persistence endowed even the blank parts
of the paper with a glow, a purity that seeped
beyond her work to the other parts of the house,
the white walls, the piles of fruit in their wooden bowl,
the patchwork quilts on our single beds, until it was all
I could see, along with her bent efforts.
We admired them, they were convincing,
almost preferable to the real thing,
filling the blanks on the wall that were wanting.

— from *The Malahat Review*

Serendipity

Téa Mutonji

Congo 1994

Congo has a song it sings each holiday
in search of more water. Men love with
their feet; like motors or ventilator.
But home—the tide meets the sunset;
they watch snipes run from the fervour.
Young boys learn to build white porches
with their hands folded into delicate pleats
They live humbly waiting on the streets

the women carry buckets of warm water—
rosemary leaves like steep tea drops on
the sand pavement road leads somewhere
inside ripe dreams and spoiled fruit. We stand—
women on top of women on top of little girls;
for their mothers flickering in between twilights
I dare to wonder still, how long until the end—
for the Okapi to rise and bow his head.

— from *Arc Poetry Magazine*

Softball team at the ferry terminal after Provincials

Kirsten Pendreigh

Their uniforms are dusty and their feet stink
but they don't want to change, not yet. Still giddy
their die-cast medals glint in the sun
as they strut the parking lot with pack strength,
cleats thrumming the asphalt. They all have ponytails,
they know that people are watching. Their fathers
pace the rows of hot cars, check coolers, call to each other
in loud voices. They can recount every hit, every missed catch.
So happy to drive, fetch ice, buy food, be needed.
When the girls get home, they'll shower for hours
retreat to their rooms. Next season, they might not sign up again.
Their cleats will still fit, but they'll be different.

— from *Room*

Stick

M Travis Lane

"Bend like water; like water bite."
Advice. But what am I?
A stick tossed on the current. I
can't bend, can't bite, can't
mark my way.

I've had my green leaves and my bloom.
Now dry, I sense the pull
of oceans I can't navigate,
nor can I choose one threaded flow
among the rocks, muds, effluent,

but like a stick a child has thrown
into a river, I bob and turn—
thrown, and thrown away.

    — from *The Walrus*

Thanks for Asking

Roxanna Bennett

   Yes, I have tried cleansing, cutting, bingeing,
purging, laughing, grieving, slutty fucking,
   cardio, physio, detoxing protocols, supplements,
surgeries, sedatives, laxatives, anti-depressants,
   anti-psychotics, hormones, opioids,
& yes turmeric, patience, positivity,
   CBT, DBT, group, art & music therapy,
outpatient, inpatient (sometimes involuntary.)
   I have 'wept & fasted, wept & prayed.'
Yes, I have tried to just get over it,
   the fragility & pain, I have tried
to explain but O god I am tired
   of the trial, of your questions,
of trying to be alive in your world.

— from *The Walrus*

This is not a monsoon poem

Manahil Bandukwala

This is infrastructure crumbling.

This is potholes
flooded with water / cars
fall in ditches / struck
run over / by
other cars

who don't see
in this / barsaat.

This is glass leaking.

This is the scar
on my foot / inch
of skin / flesh / scooped off
a slip on marble.

This is a thousand / dead / week
of pelting rain collapsed
a building.

This is schools that no longer stand,

swarms of flies / and
dengue / and not enough / vaccines
to go around.

This is the monsoon / strikes
each August.

This is crumbling.

— from *Room*

Trout Eyes
Šari Dale

The child eats trout eyes.
Like grapes, they pop

in her mouth. The skins
taste like smoke. She

likes to be seen chewing,
her lips white with oil.

Being unbearable occurs
to her. It's like music,

Eminem in Grandpa's
sauna. Brow scaled with

sweat, she trips into fire
twice before learning

to walk forward while
raking stones from sand.

Nothing has to happen,
but she questions it.

She brings beer to Uncle
and drinks lake water

on the low. On the dock,
barefoot, her mother

speaks to Sudbury loons.
The child's language

is inadequate. She sings
in English on an over-

turned tub. Someone
brings her fishing. They

call her by her sister's
name, which is a garden.

She feeds dirt to the
worms, fingernails black

brown. Uncle tosses trout
in the boat. Later he'll

burn them on the BBQ,
and someone'll pass the

child a paper plate. When
she chews, a minnow

will slip from her left ear.
The slime will stain her

tight tankini. She likely
needs a new one anyhow.

— from *The Malahat Review*

True Value

Liz Howard

The sky was never my court date.

If I died once. If I left the body.

Habeas corpus.

This is not my grave.

The value in a dead woman

is that she cannot be killed

again or cross-examined.

The value in being the dead

woman at trial is the Crown

doesn't represent you

regardless.

The value in being

dead is that it's impolite

to speak ill

of you.

What is called

wellness,

victim-witness?

A swab taken

of every orifice.

Were there any

identifying marks?

Were you in fact

on the moon

that night,

Miss Howard?

Did you make a choice?

I made a cut—it released something.

I broke the line.

— from *The Puritan*

Ways to Nurture a Name

Yohani Mendis

For all the years you butchered my name
Each letter dragged in Anglicized mud
the Sanskrit term for
blessing
felt like a dirty word
I had to scour from memory.

I tried to expunge the bad taste you left
in my mouth when
you blamed
my name
for not going easy on the tongue.

like chewing the mango's sugar off its stone
you pick at culture to cater to your palate
mine was never made for your consumption.

Still
I will teach you to say my name
until
it sticks
like honey to your lips

— from *Poetry Pause*

We Really Like Your Writing

David Romanda

Just leave us
The hell out of it
Leave your sister out too
And please
Change your name

— from *The Nashwaak Review*

What is True

Susan Musgrave

When my father said I was so useless
I couldn't boil an egg, maybe it wasn't true?
I was eleven, my mother in the hospital
having her thyroid gland removed and Dad
probably felt useless himself, blamed
his helplessness on me. Still, sixty-odd years
later his words revisit me each time I try
to work up the strength for failure
yet again, and make another meal.

My mother came home from the hospital
with a slashed throat and a new sadness.
She rose every day before we did, packed
our lunches, cooked the rolled oats we
were forced to eat. Her one complaint—
my father refused to wash the saucepan
she cooked our porridge in, left it beside
the sink for her to scrub when she came
home—he didn't approve of her working
and this was his way of wearing the pants.

We never saw the scar on our mother's throat.
She hid it under a choker of imitation pearls
and didn't wear anything she would call
revealing. What *was* useless was trying
to convince her she was beautiful, despite
the scar, or because of the scar. Yes, I see
now what is true. Because of the scar.

— from *The Malahat Review*

What Kind of Tracks Are These?

John Steffler

This morning, is the interrogative the only working gear?

Could we say it's similar to reverse because operating in
Why? or *How?* we can't clearly see where we're going or
gain much speed?

And don't we find ourselves slowly reviewing a landscape
we earlier passed through taking it in only subliminally if
at all?

And aren't we now seeing the backside of what we took for
the front?

Is it stupid to assume that the first glimpse we have of a thing
is its front?

Does looking back at the way you've come make you realize
you're lost?

Which European philosopher believed that asking questions
delays or deflects the movement of time?

Are you irritated by lists?

If you could swivel your head like an owl would reverse be
equal to forward?

Likewise, if we refuse to accumulate answers, can a barrage
of questions offer vertical lift?

Are questions inherently more comical than statements?

While a question clearly leads to a gulf that anyone might fill, is it not true that statements use their bulk or authority or menace or brutality or beauty or their intimidating confidence or blurred complexity to conceal the empty gulf behind where they started?

Do you assume there's someone inside you who could explain how you got where you are?

— from *The New Quarterly*

Yellow Tulips
Andrew DuBois

Yellow tulips so wide open they're about to fold back
on their own self, touch your own neck with the back
of your own right hand, where bottoms look like onions
in the bowl. Where did they come from? It's snowing
outside in the middle of March. One imagines where
they come from. One was only there last summer, safe
in oneself, arranging daily tulips, no snow, never will.

— from *White Wall Review*

CONTRIBUTORS' COMMENTARY
AND BIOGRAPHIES

Margaret Atwood is the author of more than fifty books published in more than forty-five countries, including works of fiction, poetry, and critical essays, as well as graphic novels. *Dearly*, her first collection of poetry in over a decade, was published in November 2020. Her most recent novel, *The Testaments,* the long-awaited sequel to *The Handmaid's Tale*, now an award-winning TV series, was a co-winner of the 2019 Booker Prize. Her fiction includes *Cat's Eye*, finalist for the 1989 Booker Prize; *Alias Grace*, which won the Giller Prize in Canada and the Premio Mondello in Italy; *The Blind Assassin*, winner of the 2000 Booker Prize; The MaddAddam Trilogy; and *Hag-Seed.* She is the recipient of the Peace Prize of the German Book Trade, the Franz Kafka International Literary Prize, the PEN Center USA Lifetime Achievement Award, and the *Los Angeles Times* Innovator's Award. She lives in Toronto.

Of "Flatline," Atwood writes: "The title comes both from the flat line that appears on a heart monitor when a person dies and the restful flat line of the horizon when you're standing on a beach looking at the ocean. At my age I've been present when a number of people have died, including my father and my mother and several good friends. When the person is in pain and not going to get better, it's hard not to see it as an escape. The poem was written before my partner, Graeme Gibson, actually died, but we both knew he was going to die quite soon. We could say the poem is about leaving one state of existence, but not necessarily in a bad way."

Ken Babstock is the author of six collections of poetry, most recently *Methodist Hatchet*, *On Malice*, and *Swivelmount* (Coach House, 2020). Twice a finalist for the Griffin Prize, he won the award in 2012 for *Methodist Hatchet*. Babstock was the inaugural recipient of the Writers' Trust Latner Prize for a body of work in mid career. He lives in Toronto with his son.

Of "Grip to Ground Connector," Babstock writes, "It's tricky finding anything to say about a list poem that isn't simply adding to the poem's list. Essentially a poem about boredom, its voice trawls back through a time of intensely long work hours in which I was intensely bored. A grip is a labourer on a film set. A labourer is a particular type in the taxonomy of workers. Grips aren't labouring while cameras roll so they sit silently on wooden boxes—risers—the technical jargon describing the rudimentary tool connecting their asses to the ground. Perhaps the last human universal is that we all have asses? We shot day for night in Queen's Park and bounced spots off a helium moon. I learned my knots from a sailing book. The best boy loitered around the jenny with his head-set off. See what I mean? I dunno, the very first set I snuck onto was Cronenberg's *Existenz*. Jude Law and Jennifer Jason Leigh walked past looking thirteen. I didn't know how things worked. I got to stand too long behind Cronenberg while holding 80 lbs of sand bag. Coming across the term *taxonomic binning* might have set the first line going, or it was the cascading list of hallucinogenic identity markers. Either way, it felt OK to collect us all up into a bundle sitting on geometric wood thinking nothing. The real money swirls round the producers."

Manahil Bandukwala is a Pakistani writer and artist based in Mississauga. She is currently completing her MA in English at the University of Waterloo. Her *Reth aur Reghistan* is a multidisciplinary literary and visual arts project that explores folklore from Pakistan. She is a member of VII, an Ottawa-based writing collective.

Bandukwala writes: "I wrote it during a trip to Karachi in 2019, my first since immigrating to Canada five years earlier. That was also the first year monsoon rains had come since I had moved out of the country. I was on a train from Islamabad to Karachi when this poem formed. We were on the last leg of our twenty-four-hour journey that became a thirty-eight-hour journey because the rains flooded the train tracks. On one hand, the monsoon breaks the desert heat, but on the other, infrastructure is not equipped to handle the severity of the rains. There's a lot of devastation that comes along with the rains. 'This is not a monsoon poem' writes against the romanticization of portrayals of monsoons in literature and media."

Courtney Bates-Hardy lives in Regina. She is the author of *House of Mystery* (2016) and a chapbook titled *Sea Foam* (2013). Her poems can be found in *Room, Carousel, This Magazine*, and the *Canadian Medical Association Journal*, among others. She is working on her second full-length collection of poetry.

Of "Knots," Bates-Hardy writes: "In the winter of 2017, I was in a car accident. This wasn't my first car accident; I had been rear-ended recently and was in two rollovers a couple years before. My body didn't recover as quickly or easily this time, and I spent the next year going through an intensive physiotherapy program. When I wrote this poem in July 2018, I was frustrated by how long it was taking to heal and imagined what it would be like if I could write my way out of the nerve pain, muscle spasms, and constant headaches. I wanted to write my way through the healing process in the same way I write through writer's block: by using free association and being flexible with language. The poem doesn't solve the problem of chronic pain, but it does say something about being open to all possibilities, even the ones that end with writer's block and nerve pain."

Roxanna Bennett gratefully resides on aboriginal land.

Of "Thanks for Asking," Bennett writes: "This poem is about the lived experience of disability."

Ronna Bloom lives in Tkaronto/Toronto. She is the author of six poetry collections. Her poems have been translated into Spanish, Bangla, and Chinese, and recorded by the CNIB. Ronna developed the Poet in Residence program at Sinai Health and is Poet in Community to the University of Toronto (ronnabloom.com).

Bloom writes: "In late 2019, I moved out of the house I'd lived in for many years. Questions of where to live and what was ok were coming from me and at me." This combined with the pre-pandemic anxiety of January 2020, when we began to brace. 'Is it Safe?' was my response to that."

Louise Carson, raised in Hudson, Quebec, has come full circle (after living elsewhere), and now makes her home with her daughter and pets in the next village over—Saint-Lazare. She studied music in Montreal and Toronto, played jazz piano, and sang in the chorus of the Canadian Opera Company. She's published twelve books, including two collections of poetry: *Dog Poems* in 2020 and *A Clearing* in 2015. When not writing, she shovels snow or gardens.

Carson writes: "Well, it's pretty obviously a love poem. I've written a few to my daughter, who, at twenty-four, is my (temporary, I know) significant other. I had her at forty, so she's only known me in middle and now old age. I had a serious illness at fifty-eight, when she was eighteen, and we both learned a lot about ourselves. Me, that all I want to do is what I have been doing: write and make her suppers. Her, that she was afraid at that time to show her emotions (love, fear) as she performed necessary medical and household tasks. 'Love you' was written two years after all that, when the drama had ended and normal life had resumed. Love you, Yaz. What would you like for supper?"

Kate Cayley lives in Toronto. She has published two collections of short stories, two collections of poetry, and a young adult novel, and written a number of plays, which have been performed in Canada, the US, and the UK. She has won the Trillium Book Award and an O Henry Prize, and has been a finalist for the Governor General's Award for Fiction, the ReLit Award for both fiction and poetry, and the K M Hunter Award.

Of "Attention," Cayley writes: "It came out of thinking about how the rhythm of household tasks might be related to poetry, to language, and to love as a repetition, a habit grown over time the way you might exercise a muscle through habitual use. I have a wife and three children. Much of our time is taken up by household tasks, which are done and then undone and done again. Loving one another, losing our tempers, finding our way back over the same local ground, this becomes a rhythm we find together. Then lose, then find. Domestic life can feel very small and constrained, and sometimes the constraint is the poetry rather than what prevents it. Emily Dickinson is in there too—she's often present for me, though her life was very different from mine. But she knew about turning what is familiar and close at hand into poetry. And that got me to praise: the hypothesis that language was sung before it was spoken. Song always feels like a form of praise. Praise is also involved in marriage and in being with children, and how we must praise one another, and forget how to, and then remember."

Kitty Cheung is a Chinese Canadian writer living and creating on ancestral Coast Salish lands. Currently an undergraduate student at Simon Fraser University, she studies interactive arts and technology with a minor in world literature. Through storytelling, she is interested in exploring the overlap between cultural identity, queerness, and mental health. Her poems, essays, and arts reviews have been published in *The Peak SFU*, *The Lyre*, and *Ricepaper Magazine*.

Cheung writes: "Ma's husband has this ridiculous shot glass. He must have bought it from a tourist shop in downtown Vancouver shortly after immigrating. 'bikini tits shot glass' is an attempt to jab at the sexism and colonial patriotism behind this object that sits on our dining table. The shot glass provides a succinct and stinging symbol of what my stepdad's presence has brought into our family. I wanted to dissect and document my response as an immigrant's daughter in a Cantonese-speaking household: there's disbelief, there's indignance, there's drama. There's a frustration at the lack of understanding as mother-daughter conversations fumble between Cantonese and English. There's a feeling of screaming across a chasm of language, cultural, and generational barriers, only to be met with echoes of disappointment. How do you reconcile Ma's dream of a nuclear family as her new husband tramples into your home? How do you articulate these feelings to her when you never fully share a language?"

Dani Couture lives in Toronto. Her collection *Listen Before Transmit* (Wolsak & Wynn) came out in 2018.

Of "Driver's Ed at 41," Couture writes: "This poem offers two possibilities at the end: to continue or not to. The poem, in part, addresses how one can do both, sometimes for years on end. The lines address a personal collapse of time and memory. How twenty-five years ago can feel closer than a week ago and how tomorrow can feel nearly impossible until you find yourself a day past it looking back."

Kayla Czaga lives in Victoria, British Columbia, where she teaches poetry online and works in a pizzeria. She is the author of *For Your Safety Please Hold On* (Nightwood Editions, 2014) and *Dunk Tank* (House of Anansi, 2019), which was shortlisted for the BC/Yukon Book Prizes' Dorothy Livesay Poetry Prize. "The Peace Lily" is her fifth poem to be chosen for the *Best Canadian Poetry* series.

Czaga writes: "I wrote the opening line of 'The Peace Lily' on the top of the Thrifty Foods receipt right after I bought the plant. I didn't know it would die yet or take such a long time doing so. I just liked the music of, 'The peace lily I bought at Thrifty Foods for $4.99 taught me something.' I begin a lot of poems on scraps of paper: backs of receipts, the margins of my serving notepads, bill envelopes. I didn't go back to the line for a long time; the receipt stayed crumpled up in my wallet for months. Eventually, I dug it out while I was cleaning out my purse. By that time, the peace lily was well into its dying and had actually taught me something. For me, writing is often an aggravating game of patience. I begin a lot of poems that take years to ripen and develop what they're about. Like plants from the grocery store, sometimes I don't know what colour their flowers are going to be, or if they are even going to flower. Maybe they're fruit trees. Maybe they'll just have pretty leaves. I just water them from time to time and hope. Or I neglect them, but they grow anyway, like this poem. A lot of times they just wither up and die, but sometimes they survive and become something."

Šari Dale is a Judaeo-Czech settler from Prince George, British Columbia, on the unceded ancestral lands of the Lheidli T'enneh. She holds a BA in English and Creative Writing from the University of British Columbia Okanagan. Her poetry has been published in *Arc*, *Grain*, and *The Malahat Review* among others.

Of "Trout Eyes," Dale writes: "This piece came out of a conversation I had with my dear friend and fellow poet Ashleigh

Giffen. We were driving around telling each other stories from our childhoods in rural Canada, and I asked her if she'd ever eaten a fish eye, which she hadn't. As a little girl, I always ate eyes from the fish my family caught at Joe Lake near Sudbury, Ontario. I didn't like the taste as much as I liked grossing out my relatives. That memory stuck with me, though the poem became more about experiencing the world without having the language to properly explain it. Back then, I wanted to understand why things were the way they were. What did adults know that made them adults? I couldn't see the 'logical' connections between things, and, somehow, that made them seem all the more miraculous."

Unnati Desai is a student from Ontario. She has been published in *Room* magazine.

Of "an ode to my brother's forehead stitches," Desai writes: "The poem was inspired by a time in our childhood when my brother was trying to follow me and fell onto his forehead. He did not shed a single tear until I turned around to see blood gushing down his face and screamed, 'Blood!'"

Tina Do lives and works on the unceded traditional and ancestral territories of the Coast Salish peoples of the Səlilwətaɬ (Tsleil-Waututh), Skwxwú7mesh (Squamish), Kwikwitlem and xʷməθkwəy̓əm (Musqueam) Nations. She is currently an MA student at Simon Fraser University. She was honoured with her first publication credit through *The /tɛmz/ Review*, and longlisted for the CBC Poetry Prize in 2020.

Of "i tell my mother everything," Do writes: "This piece came to be after I received a bit of bad news. Though I shared the news with close friends and my sister, the thought of telling my mother never once crossed my mind. Strangely enough, I do not know when I stopped sharing parts of my life with her. What I realized soon after, however, was that my mother and I have spent two decades dancing around each other; though we talk, we never say anything substantial.

I bring up my childhood piano, which we had to sell in order to make space and pay rent, but I never told my mother how much it hurt having to say goodbye to it. The poem confesses things I have kept to myself for years, while also working through what it means to be a daughter of immigrant parents. There are things I still wrestle with and try to reconcile with myself, including the responsibility of helping my mother navigate the English language. As I grow older, I wonder if having a relationship with my mother is a positive thing, especially when being in her presence makes me feel unmoored."

Andrew DuBois lives in Carbonear, Newfoundland. He is proprietor of the Green Door Book Store and a professor at the University of Toronto. Some of his books include *Ashbery's Forms of Attention*, *The Anthology of Rap*, *Close Reading: The Reader*, and *Start to Figure: Fugitive Essays, Selected Reviews*, which contains reviews of roughly two hundred books of contemporary Canadian poetry. "Yellow Tulips" appears in a volume called *All the People Are Pregnant*.

Of "Yellow Tulips," DuBois writes: "About two decades ago I tagged along through the museums of Europe with a lover and friend who studied medieval Netherlandish art—specifically Depositions and the way their fabrics, the robes of patrons and mourners painted on the wooden panels of devotional diptychs and triptychs, folded: creased and shadowed and sharded. This person also studied puppets. We were in Amsterdam for three months and there were tulips everywhere. Years later I was alone in the midst of another interminable winter and, looking out the window, I erased the snow in my mind and saw myself sitting again outside the Coffeeshop La Tertulia, in the summer Dutch sun, nibbling some banana bread freshly baked by the mother and daughter owners, sipping an Americano, fingering a robust beautiful tulip, and watching the boats glide down the canals. I hugged myself warm and wrote this poem."

Paola Ferrante lives in Toronto. Her first poetry collection, *What to Wear When Surviving a Lion Attack* (Mansfield Press, 2019) was shortlisted for the Gerald Lampert Memorial Award. Her poetry won the 2020 Short *Grain* Writing Contest, and her fiction won *The New Quarterly*'s Peter Hinchcliffe Award, *Room*'s Fiction Contest, and was longlisted for the 2020 Journey Prize. Her work is forthcoming in *CV2* and *North American Review* and she is the poetry editor at *Minola Review*.

Of "Asch's Line Study in the Current Anthropocene," Ferrante writes: "When I wrote this poem, I was feeling a lot of grief around the climate crisis, along with guilt about the ways my life has contributed to it. In undergrad, I studied psychology and Asch's line study is one of those classic studies in conformity that still stuck with me, years and years later. In the study, the subject is shown a line of a certain length and asked which line matches it best. And even though it was an unambiguous answer, (line C), people still chose the wrong line, B, because the confederates of the experimenter all chose that line. So I remember thinking about the pressures in conforming to a capitalist system, along with the poetic possibilities of choosing to 'be' and simply continuing to live the way we do, rather than 'see' the issues we're creating which contribute to a climate emergency. This is a poem of mourning, but also a call to action. It is a recognition of how all of us are implicated in the current climate crisis, and how we need to wake up to this in order to have a future, especially for the next generation."

Beth Goobie lives in Saskatoon and is the author of twenty-five books. Her poetry collection, *breathing at dusk,* received two 2018 Sask Book Awards. A new collection, *Lookin' for Joy,* will be published by Exile Editions in 2022. It was gratefully written on a SK Arts grant. Beth lives in Saskatoon.

Goobie writes, "'Civilization lives in the throat' was written as part of a collection funded by a SK Arts grant. For one year, I was granted the financial sanctuary to wait, day after day with pen in hand, for a poem to grace my consciousness. The joy of writing poetry is that each and every line can go anywhere. With fiction, your options narrow as you progress; with poetry, they celebrate first and last lines with equal abandon. While the overarching theme of the collection dealt with seeking joy in the uncertainty of aging, each poem was its own particular queendom. I find that poems write me, and my job as author is to watch myself change on the page. 'Civilization lives in the throat' is a continual shapeshifting, from the auditory to the kinetic to the visual, etc—an unplanned process wherein each image stepped out of itself into a free-flow of form. I could only have written this poem later on in life, when I had grown more accustomed to the alchemical reflection in the mirror and a deepening knowing in the bones. A primary constant throughout my writing career from the beginning, however, has been financial support from various arts organisations, both provincial and federal. Thank you from the depths of my bones!"

Nina Philomena Honorat is a poet and writer born in Montreal who has honed her skills in poetry slams, workshops, and the occasional poetry night in Rheims (France), Amherst (USA), and Toronto (Canada). She is an associate editor for *Juniper: A Poetry Journal*. Currently, she's working on developing a multi-media installation project and growing the most colourful garden in her backyard.

Of "Reckoning," Honorat writes: "When I wrote this poem at the end of 2019, it felt like the end of the world. As if I'd only heard bad news for months and that things were only worsening, here and abroad, for everyone. In my personal life, I was also recovering from a lot of heavy blows to my ego: burnouts at work, broken relationships, lack of motivation. I was wrestling with ideas, projects, and themes I had never fully developed due to soul-crushing writer's block. With a sudden burst of creativity, I tried to capture the illusive and abrupt feeling of 'before' and 'after,' a transformation both necessary and agonizing. Ultimately, I was looking to vocalize the dread and apprehension I felt in that moment, attempting to do so through indications of sound or its absence."

Liz Howard was born and raised on Treaty 9 territory in Northern Ontario and currently lives in Toronto. Her debut collection, *Infinite Citizen of the Shaking Tent*, won the 2016 Griffin Poetry Prize and was shortlisted for the 2015 Governor General's Award for Poetry. Her second collection, *Letters in a Bruised Cosmos*, will be published in June 2021 by McClelland & Stewart. She is of mixed settler and Anishinaabe heritage.

Of "True Value," Howard writes: "This is a poem about trading your life to keep living. A poem about living, regardless. A poem about taking comfort in how a lake reflects the sky. The double bind of what it is to testify. A poem about refusing the hook that finds you. A poem about breaking the line that might have found you caught."

Maureen Hynes lives in Toronto, and has published five books of poetry. Her most recent is *Sotto Voce*, a finalist for the Golden Crown Award in poetry for lesbian writers (US) and the Pat Lowther Award. Her first book won the League of Canadian Poets' Gerald Lampert Award, and other collections have been shortlisted for the Raymond Souster Award, and the Pat Lowther Award. This is her third appearance in the *Best Canadian Poetry* series.

Of "All clear," Hynes writes: "For me, a phrase or line from another poet often sparks an idea, forms a springboard to leap into a poem. In this case, I had been rereading the poetry of Lorine Niedecker in a course led by Hoa Nguyen, and one of the lines in Niedecker's long poem 'Progression' about the arrival of spring struck me: 'It comes out in March by the back fence, the full / and true Relation of the present State of new country / and the coming of the world green.' In that particular spring of 2020, there was *a lot* coming out, not just 'the green,' and not just by the back fence. This poem reflects the very early days of the pandemic, when, like many others, I hauled out my elderly sewing machine and began stitching masks—the activity itself a kind of shield against fear and anxiety. Months before the pandemic had begun, I'd been having tests for a fearful medical condition; the onset of the pandemic delayed appointments with doctors and getting results. This sonnet expresses mostly relief, but also gratitude to the doctor who relayed positive news to me over the phone. And who also asked how my poetry was going, a great kindness in the heightened fraughtness of those early days."

George K Ilsley is from Nova Scotia and has lived in Vancouver for many years. His memoir, *The Home Stretch: A Father, a Son, and All the Things They Never Talk About*, was published in 2020. He is the author of *ManBug* (novel) and *Random Acts of Hatred* (short fiction), and has won writing contests for fiction, creative non-fiction, and most recently, for poetry, in Dawson City, Yukon, in which he was paid in gold.

Of "Another Woman in Canada," George writes: "When Alice Munro won the Nobel Prize in Literature in 2013, her work came to the attention of many new readers. Some started with her most recent book, *Dear Life* (McClelland & Stewart, 2012), and they were not impressed. Reviews reveal the reviewer. Revealed here are ignorance, unintentional irony, and a disdain for Canadians and the qualities of ordinary life—the sort of life the vast majority of us tend to experience. These reviews also display a blinkered worldview where 'the big literary prize' must be a Pulitzer (the cultural elite know that Alice Munro could never win a Pulitzer, which is only awarded to US writers). Fans of Alice Munro and those inside the CanLit universe nourish their own biases. It is painful to see the beloved short stories of our Nobel Laureate so brutally dismissed. Canadian readers can't imagine not knowing who Alice Munro is, can't imagine not appreciating her work, can't imagine not discovering thrilling new fiction in *The New Yorker*. If you are familiar with the contents of *Dear Life* you may feel even more protective of dear Alice, because this collection includes stories that Munro, ever so generous, tells us are as close to memoir as anything she will ever write."

Eve Joseph lives in Victoria and works on the unceded territory of the Lekwungen people. Her three books of poetry were all nominated for the Dorothy Livesay Award. *In the Slender Margin*, published by HarperCollins in 2014, won the Hubert Evans Non-Fiction Prize. Her most recent book of poetry, *Quarrels*, won the 2019 Griffin Prize.

Joseph writes: "As with most of my prose poems, 'family history' is an amalgam of truth and fiction. At some point, during the pandemic, I was going through an old file folder of notes and letters and I found an email from a cousin in Israel (whom I've never met) asking if I knew that my grandfather had tried to cut his brother's throat and that his mother did bring him a chicken as a substitute! Honestly, you can't make these things up. For me, the absurd is a doorway into broader philosophical musings. The 'story' itself is cushioned between thoughts about time, forgetfulness, and memory. When it was published in *The Malahat*, the editor commented on how the poem echoed the story of God commanding Abraham to sacrifice his son . . . and the ram that was offered as a substitute. I did not write the piece with this biblical reference in mind; however, in the process of writing a poem, everything that we know—whether conscious or unconscious—comes into play and can enter the work."

Ian Keteku is a Ghanaian-Canadian writer and multimedia artist based out of Tkaronto. He is the 2010 World Poetry Slam Champion and is the author of *Black Abacus* (Write Bloody North, 2019). Keteku teaches in the creative writing program at OCAD University.

Of "Mango," Keteku writes: "My father's life is most likely in its final season. Kidney disease has rendered him dependent on regular dialysis. Nowadays, all he can speak of is Africa and how he yearns to go back. We, his children, know it would be a one-way trip. As I struggled with this reality—the question of whether to keep my father in Canada with access to stable health care or grant him his wish of returning to Ghana, so he could embrace the air for one last time—I wrote this poem."

Judith Krause is a Regina poet, a former Saskatchewan Poet Laureate, and author of five poetry collections and a collaborative chapbook. She completed an MFA at Warren Wilson College and has been awarded residencies and fellowships in the US and France. Her work has appeared in print or online in Canada, the US, and Ireland. She is at work on a sixth collection.

Of "Day of the Dead," Krause writes: "The first year after my mother died, every holiday, every birthday or special occasion that we would have celebrated together, was a painful reminder she was gone. I found myself looking for ways to keep her alive—hanging paintings of her beloved Qu'Appelle Valley in my office, my bathroom, and my bedroom, using her tablecloths for family dinners, and planting her favorite flowers in my garden. My mother's father was a cancer specialist who died when she was in her teens, and she was haunted by his loss all her life. As she aged, her fascination with death grew, as has mine. And yes, even though it's been more than a few years, those sweaters are still hanging on the laundry rack."

M Travis Lane came from the US to Fredericton, New Brunswick with her husband, Lauriat Lane Jr, and infant daughter Hannah in 1960. Their son, Lauriat Lane III, was born here. The family became Canadian citizens in 1973.

Of "Stick," Lane writes: "Widowed, I live with an elderly blind cat and with assistance from friends and family. Old age has its incapacities and its glum moments, which the poem represents."

Mary Dean Lee lives in Montreal and is a professor emeritus at McGill University. Her poetry has appeared recently in *Hamilton Arts & Letters*, *The Tishman Review*, *The Halcyone*, *The Write Launch*, *Event*, *Grain*, and *Montréal Serai*. She grew up in Milledgeville, Georgia, studied theatre and literature at Duke University and Eckerd College, and received her PhD in organizational behavior at Yale University.

Of "Riddle," Lee writes: "It came to me after I had written several poems about my brother's car accident at age seventeen, after which he lived for two and a half years with massive brain damage and then died. I realized I wanted to try to capture the effects of this tragedy on my whole family: my other brother, me, and my mother and father. My other brother, who was fourteen and living at home when the accident happened, was closer to the crisis than I was, since I had already gone away to university. When he was nineteen, he cut off communications with the family for seven years."

Canisia Lubrin is a writer, editor, and teacher who creates in Whitby, Ontario. She is the author of *Voodoo Hypothesis* (2017), and *The Dyzgraph*^{x}*st* (M&S, 2020), winner of the 2021 OCM Bocas Prize for Caribbean Poetry, the 2021 Griffin Poetry Prize, and the 2021 Derek Walcott Poetry Prize, and longlisted for the Pat Lowther and Raymond Souster awards. Lubrin is a 2021 Windham-Campbell poetry laureate. Her fiction debut, *Code Noir*, is forthcoming from Knopf Canada.

Of "In the Middle of the Burning," Lubrin writes: "The poem contemplates the early days of the 2020 Black Lives Matter uprisings following the death of George Floyd and Breonna Taylor (and, sadly in a naturalized order, others) during the ongoing COVID-19 pandemic. I had been speaking with a poet friend about what it means to be (poets) committed to the difficult subjects of our lives, of our world. As the year lengthened by the state of the world growing darker, time made little of its usual (no doubt, forced) sense. Does a poet—such as I am—feel continually called upon to make sense of things? When, through most of those tumultuous days, everything seemed too overwhelming for language and I assumed everyone else was living in the same difficult world, the inevitable questions about the further clarified inequities of this world led me to this poem. In the midst of all the continuing disillusionments—increased surveillance of our lives, and the ruling class' highly organized attempts to co-opt and curtail demands for a better world for us all—I reached for language that I hoped could gesture to how to continue to extend the generosity of ourselves in every direction. Even, and especially, after the poem ends."

Randy Lundy is a Cree, Irish, and Norwegian member of the Barren Lands First Nation. He was born in Thompson, Manitoba, grew up in Hudson Bay, Saskatchewan, and has lived in Treaty 4 territory in Saskatchewan for more than twenty years now. Randy has published four books of poetry, most recently *Blackbird Song* (2018) and *Field Notes for the Self* (2020) with URegina Press, where he is editor for the *Oskana Poetry and Poetics* series.

Of "Morning Pages," Lundy writes: "The poem is transparent about its own sources. It begins with a solitary persona in a particular setting, and then moves into the persona's thoughts: first, the simile 'like smoke from a bush fire' transitions the reader into a story about a cousin; second, we read of 'an article' the character has been reading, before the poem makes a reference to cosmology and physics, and then names 'violence' as a central concern; third, there is a leaping transition to a memory / story from the persona's workplace and an experience with colleagues, which raises the issue of intercultural learning and relations, or the failure of such; finally, there is a hackneyed joke before the poem concludes with a reference to Auden's famous line 'poetry makes nothing happen' and comes to a close with an image of a world that carries on in the absence of anything human. If the poem is a kind of collage of memories and stories, then it seems the challenge for the reader is to ask and then attempt some provisional answer to the question, *How do these various parts fit together?* For me, the poem is straight-up autobiography. Here's some stuff I was thinking about one day. The title comes from something a clever reader said of my recent work, that it read to her like 'morning pages,' which I take to be the product of someone simply writing down their thoughts each morning to keep themselves in the practice of writing."

David Ly lives in Vancouver. He is the author of *Mythical Man*, which was shortlisted for a 2021 ReLit Award. David also wrote the chapbook *Stubble Burn*. His sophomore poetry collection, *Dream of Me as Water*, is forthcoming with Palimpsest Press/Anstruther Books in 2022. David is the poetry editor for *This Magazine*, part of the Anstruther Press editorial collective, and a poetry manuscript consultant at SFU's The Writers' Studio.

Ly writes: "Like a lot of my poems, 'Memory of the Black Lake,' was written after dwelling on an image for weeks before writing anything down. I imagined mermaids in a lake and asked myself why they would be there, so I made up this idea that these particular mermaids would come in from the ocean through some sort of underwater passage in order to spawn. Then, the addition of two boys rowing onto the lake was a way for me to show this image I had been stuck with. It then developed into an exploration of not only a mysterious setting, but also the uncertainties of a (new) relationship. It also took on new life when I titled it as a 'memory.' I thought about how people may have different recollections of the same event. So, 'Memory of the Black Lake' turned into just one perspective of what happened on the lake. I can't wait to hopefully publish the perspective of the other character in this poem. I really like building small, tight stories into my poems with simple language, and I am proud of how this one did that."

Yohani Mendis lives in Toronto. Her writing received an honourable mention in the 2020 Edna Staebler Personal Essay Contest and placed second in the 2021 Toronto International Festival of Authors/Fan Expo Flash Fiction Contest. Her creative nonfiction essays have appeared in various journals and anthologies, including *The New Quarterly*, *The Hart House Review*, and *Watch Your Head*. "Ways to Nurture a Name," which appeared in *Poetry Pause*, is her first published poem.

Of "Ways to Nurture a Name," Yohani writes: "My first name is not Yohani—it is a middle name—and my last name is not Mendis. My real first and last name is Bhagya Manukulasuriya. I grew up in a predominantly European expat community in Bahrain and went to a European high school. As a child, I harboured a lot of self-hatred and one of the many things I turned upon was my name. When you're young, and numerous (white) authority figures repeatedly demean your identity, it wears on you. I've heard it all: from instructors calling me a variety of terms they found amusing, to the editor-in-chief at a daily news agency, where I undertook a reporting job, advising me to use a pen name for my bylines because it was 'easier on the tongue.' This poem, written in my mid-twenties and during a period of great emotional displacement, was in direct response to those sort of people—the ones who dub themselves progressives and yet thrive under the neocolonial conditions they sow and reap for themselves, including that of cultural imperialism. In this poem, the speaker searches for inner acceptance, amidst internalized racism. The defiant resolution she arrives at, albeit exhausted, is a reclamation of the sweetness inherent in her cultural heritage and identity."

Pamela Mosher lives in Ottawa, and was born and raised in rural Nova Scotia. Her writing has recently been published in *Juniper*, *Grain*, and *Literary Mama*. She lives with her wife and their two young children, and works as a technical writer.

Of "On Artificially Conceiving our Children," Mosher writes: "This poem began as a sort of bristling response to some of the loaded language that surrounds motherhood—including 'natural,' with its implication of 'normal' and 'best' and 'correct' and all the associated social judgement. Then it expanded into a way for me to process and make peace with my own experience of conceiving my daughter—of the medicalization of it, and how for me as a gay woman, that *was* what was normal, or typical. Eventually, the poem developed into a consideration of my children and their perspectives, since the experience of parenthood is as much about the new people brought into the world as it is about the changed lives of those who become parents. I am moved by the way young children don't apply a moral weight to their considerations. They live in each moment, and care about the fundamentals—that they are loved, that they are fed, that they are having fun."

Susan Musgrave lives on Haida Gwaii, islands in the North Pacific that lie equidistant from Luxor, Machu Picchu, Ninevah, and Timbuktu. The high point of her literary career was finding her name in the index of *Montreal's Irish Mafia*. Her new book of poetry, *Exculpatory Lilies*, will be published by M&S in 2022.

Of "What is True," Musgrave writes: "This poem contends with family dynamics, those that smoulder, like underground fires; fed by a little bit of oxygen they can burn for centuries. My father really did say to me, 'You're so useless you can't boil an egg'; with mum in the hospital I think he felt useless himself, and took his fear and his frustration out on me. All these years later when I begin to make a meal, I still hear his words. Even though I am a good cook, my father's words endorse my inner critic, who says, 'This time it won't turn out. You will fail.' Malcolm Lowry wrote, 'Fear ringed by doubt is my eternal moon.' Perhaps this could be every writer's motto? You can never be 'perfect' when it comes to writing. So those of us who feel deeply flawed are drawn to a profession where we are doomed, in some sense, never to be 'good enough.' I had lunch a few years ago with two friends, one a smouldering hot underground fire of a woman from Newfoundland, the other a gangster-turned-writer and philosopher. Angelina, whose father was in the military, said he used to call her ugly, homely; Donny, who is one of the smartest men I know, had a father who was a drunk, and called him stupid. I said we should start a service called 'Ugly, Stupid, and Useless: Family Therapy and Counselling.' We would have made a killing."

Téa Mutonji is an Afro-Canadian writer from Scarborough, currently attending school in New York City. Her first collection of short stories, *Shup Up You're Pretty* (VS. Books/ Arsenal Pulp Press) was shortlisted for the Atwood Gibson Writers' Trust Fiction Prize and won the Edmund White Award and the Trillium Book Award.

Of "Serendipity," Mutonji writes: "It was Professor Daniel Tysdal who had introduced our class to Wanda Campbell. Her work was full of discipline and intention and welcome. My poetry has always been pretty prosy, free verse and confessional. We were given the assignment to respond to Campbell's collection by engaging with the content of the work or responding to the form. These poems were about India and Chile, the countries, the cities, the streets becoming their own characters. Campbell's book was called *Kalamkari & Cordillera* and the poems were written in rows and in column and could be read from left to right, or top to bottom. I had never read anything like it. And in fact, I wasn't a big form writer to begin with. The act of reading was so interactive, immersive. I thought of the word 'serendipity' before I began writing my own response. That's how it made me feel. Like I could exist in two places at once, or that one place could be multiplied. I felt that way all my life in Canada, even though I immigrated at a young age. Like I was here, and I was also there. Thinking this way incites my practice. I start with a word, a feeling, a truth. Around that time, I was learning more about my country, the Democratic Republic of the Congo. I was watching documentaries about life there, about a place called 'City of Joy,' where women who had survived sexual assault could go to heal, could go to forgive. I was reading about Dandies, about La Sape, a way of life that's meant to promote what we call 'Joie de vivre.' And this was all happening in the same place that is suffering from civil unrest, poverty, exploitation. I thought, how wonderful, to reach for light in a place like this. I was remembering or imagining Congo like how I left it, a place where people take their experiences and carry it on their backs, posture tall, shoulders raised—That's my Congo, that's my 1994."

Barbara Nickel lives in Yarrow, British Columbia, on the Stó:lo territory of the Pilalt and Ts'elxwéyeqw tribes. Her poetry book *Essential Tremor* was released in Spring 2021. Her first collection, *The Gladys Elegies*, won the Pat Lowther Award and another, *Domain*, was a *Quill & Quire* Best Book of the Year. Her work has appeared in many publications, including *The Walrus* and *Poetry Ireland Review*. Nickel is also an award-winning author of books for young people.

Nickel writes: "'Essential Tremor' is one of two title poems in my newly released collection. The first 'Essential Tremor' was written years ago as a portrait poem of my parents-in-law, the caregiving of one spouse for another suffering from multiple health issues, including the neurological condition called essential tremor, which is uncontrolled shaking without a known cause. I wrote the poem from a relatively objective distance, and was intrigued with the name given to the condition, enough for 'Essential Tremor' to become the working title of my manuscript-in-progress, an exploration of many bodies' disruptions. Several years later, my husband was diagnosed with a neurological illness and the tremor, as it were, moved into my own bed. This poem is my working-through of the diagnosis. Like its earlier companion, this 'Essential Tremor' is a sonnet. The form seemed to embody not only the constraints of a caregiver's perspective and role, but also the gifts, like the frictions of slant rhyme echoing the tiny movements of the tremor itself. Although written years apart, both poems wanted to begin and end with an image of a hand."

Ottavia Paluch is a high school senior from Mississauga, Ontario. Her writing has been published or is forthcoming in *Four Way Review, Tinderbox Poetry Journal,* and *Ghost City Review*, among other places. She is an alumna of the *Adroit Journal* Summer Mentorship Program, *Flypaper Lit*'s Flight School workshop, and the Iowa Young Writers Studio.

Of "Re: That One Part of My Brain That Will Never Leave Me Alone," Paluch writes: "During the first week of one of my compulsory English classes, we were assigned the task of writing a creative piece on something we dealt with in our lives. We were allowed to be as broad or narrow in scope as we felt was necessary while also managing to stay within a two-page limit. It was a diagnostic of sorts, a means of gauging our ability to string sentences together cohesively. English is one of my favourite subjects, and as an avid reader and writer, I felt that the task at hand was right up my alley. I proceeded to write a two-page first draft of 'Re . . .' Writing this poem was my attempt to understand what exactly was going on in my brain in a way that was rooted less in science and more in emotion and personal memory. It went through many rounds of revision, during which I kept the lines I felt were most impactful and got rid of everything else. This poem was important to my development as a writer and poet, and I have come a long way since writing it. It acted as early proof that what I had to say could connect with people, and for that I will always be grateful."

Kirsten Pendreigh is a poet and children's author from BC. Her poems appear in magazines like *Arc Poetry, Prairie Fire,* and *subTerrain,* and in the anthologies *Sweet Water: Poems for the Watersheds* (Caitlin Press), *Sustenance* (Anvil Press), *Another Dysfunctional Cancer Poem Anthology* (Mansfield Press), and *The / temz / Review Covid-19 Anthology.* Kirsten has children's picture books forthcoming in 2022 and 2023, and hopes to put a poetry manuscript out in the world soon.

Of "Softball team at the ferry terminal after Provincials," Pendreigh writes: "I wanted to show the undercurrent of awareness parents of teens share—that the window of time with their child is closing. My daughter and her 'Wildcats' softball team began playing in grade four and stuck together all through high school. While I didn't love sitting on cold metal bleachers, waiting in hot cars at ferry terminals, or finding stinky socks festering in bags, I loved watching those girls play ball. As they grew and changed, end-of-season left me wondering how many would return next year. Sadly, girls quit sports at much higher rates than boys. So, I wanted to talk about the power girls get to experience as athletes and team-mates. Power they're often denied in other parts of their lives. Do they sense that it's fleeting? Is that why they sign up again? Can they carry that strength with them, when they move on?"

Emily Pohl-Weary lives on unceded Musqueam territory in Vancouver. She's the award-winning author of seven books, including the poetry collection *Ghost Sick* and the young adult novel *Not Your Ordinary Wolf Girl.* An inveterate genre-hopper, her previous books include a ghost love story, a middle-grade mystery, a biography, a superhero anthology, and a girl-pirate comic. Emily teaches creative writing at the University of British Columbia and is writing a new novel and an audio play.

Of "Dawson," Pohl-Weary writes: "This poem was written while I was at Berton House in Dawson City, Yukon, the year after my marriage fell apart. Until that time, I'd always lived within twenty square blocks of west-end Toronto, worked seven days a week, and was having constant panic attacks. In a frenzy of needing to reduce my anxiety and be anywhere but home, I applied to writing residencies across the country. Amazingly, I was selected for four of them. These short-term jobs took me from the west coast to the east coast and also up north. I was very nervous about moving to Dawson City for a summer—all I knew was that the gold rush and *Call of the Wild* happened there—and had no clue what to pack. To my surprise, instead of being a lonely city girl, I was immediately welcomed into a community of hardy, creative, down-to-earth people. They helped me get back in touch with what made me happy. I wrote poetry, made new friends, drove north of the Arctic Circle, read a lot of comics, hiked in the tundra, spent part of each day in nature, picked more wild berries than I could eat, got invited to stay at the off-grid Tr'ondëk Hwëch'in Camp called Land of Plenty, and went dancing at least once a week. By the end of that year of travel and impermanence, I was no longer having back-to-back panic attacks. Then I was offered a job at UBC, and moved away from Toronto for the foreseeable future."

David Romanda was born in Kelowna, British Columbia and currently lives in Kawasaki City, Japan. His chapbook, *I'm Sick of Pale Blue Skies*, was published in Spring 2021 (Ethel Press).

Of "We Really Like Your Writing," Romanda writes: "A poem of mine upset my parents. The offending poem, in my mind, had nothing to do with any member of the family. This was my response to the situation."

Matthew Rooney was born in Vancouver and grew up in Halifax. Last year, he completed his MA in English at Dalhousie University. Rooney has published a dozen (or so) works of poetry, two short stories, a few literary essays, and one entomological study. He is currently working on drafts of what he hopes will be his first published collection of poetry.

Rooney writes: "It's a rare poem, at least for me, in that it came the way poems are fabled to come. In the summer of 2019 I travelled to Newfoundland for three weeks to visit my partner. I remember, during that time, the weather being uncharacteristically stable. We were able to do a lot of hiking in those weeks. Skerwink Trail (in Trinity East) was particularly striking. We spent hours watching whales and seagulls navigate the rocky outcrops. I had also, around this time, become interested in forms of Chinese poetry—particularly forms that have four-line stanzas, where each line has a strict number of characters. In an attempt to understand the forms better, I tried writing some poems in English with similar restrictions, substituting Chinese characters for English syllables. 'Seagulls' came to me, in its first draft, as I attempted to describe the landscape of Skerwink with the formal restrictions of Chinese-inspired syllabic poetry. The poem attempts to present an image of the Skerwink landscape in a way that demonstrates the subjective, human perspective, and in a way that demonstrates this perspective without a speaker. I did not want to describe the image, but to present it through human constructs."

Zoe Imani Sharpe lives in Tkarón:to/Toronto. She is a poet, essayist, editor, and facilitator. Her recent work is forthcoming in *CV2*.

Sharpe writes: "Wanda Coleman, Jan Beatty, and Lorine Niedecker are only a few, though important, examples of poets who write or wrote about the intricate web of economic pressure within which poets might find themselves. In my time, this web has its own particularities, both inside and outside what might be called the Art World (which is actually many 'worlds'—including Poetry Worlds). This acknowledgement was one motivation for writing 'Loss +': how *does* a poet make a living through the writing of [her] life? Poetry is as exciting a form as it is baffling (the sheer flexibility of the thing!). This flexibility is why poetry's mathematical and exchange/value properties continue to intrigue, especially in the case of poems that come directly out of conditions of broke-ness. I tried to create a preliminary web of concepts in relation to the material that is money: oscillation, static. I sensed an absence of both thought and discussion, in Canada, about the lack of value placed on the one who declares [her] value through the writing of poetry. Still, I carry a deep uncertainty about the very meaning and utility of this word, 'value.' There is a lot more to say about this, of course. These days I find myself asking, as many poets do: how does poetic language, which is sometimes also economic language, operate on a material level? I hope this poem invites readers to activate the potential energy of these questions."

Sue Sinclair lives in Fredericton, on Wolastoqiyik Territory, where she teaches at the University of New Brunswick and edits for *The Fiddlehead* and Brick Books. She is the author of five collections of poetry, all of which have won or have been nominated for national and/or regional awards. Her most recent book, *Heaven's Thieves,* won the 2017 Pat Lowther Award, and her *New and Selected* is forthcoming from Goose Lane Editions. Sue has a PhD in philosophy and wrote her dissertation on the subject of beauty.

Of "The Peonies," Sinclair writes: "I love peonies, the big, poufy cultivars in particular. But I also come from the kind of cultural background that inclines me to see such beings as, well, a bit much. Precisely because of this, I'm curious about the virtues of being a bit much. I didn't set out to write the poem with that thought in mind, but it's not surprising that it became one of the poem's primary energies. It's also not surprising to see beauty creeping into the poem, because although I wrote my dissertation on beauty some years ago, it continues to be a preoccupation. I'm interested in experiences that invite questions about beauty, its difficulties and possibilities. Peonies—which my once-housemate planted in our front yard years ago—are one of these points of questioning."

John Steffler lives in rural Eastern Ontario. He has published seven books of poems, two novels, and a book of essays about poetry, language, and wilderness (*Forty-One Pages*, University of Regina Press, 2019). His most recent collection of poems is *And Yet* (McClelland & Stewart, 2020). From 2006 to 2009 he was Parliamentary Poet Laureate of Canada.

Steffler writes: "I usually rework poems over a period of months, but I wrote 'What Kind of Tracks Are These?' more or less at a single sitting. The thinking in the poem had been going on in the back of my mind for a long time. I'd been thinking about approaching writing as a kind of reading—a reading of experiences, memories, the surrounding world as an array of signs, the way I might try to read the tracks left by some unseen creature. This approach to writing would be more receptive than assertive, more a matter of listening and observing, less a matter of claiming territory with loud words. It would involve questioning and discovering what *is*—what is real—rather than overlaying the world with wishful thinking or inventing alternative worlds. Following clues, piecing together causes and backstories helps us understand who we are, where things have come from, and where they might be heading. Don't questions invite surprise? And doesn't the downfall of an oppressive old custom or structure often start with a bold, original question?

Sarah Yi-Mei Tsiang lives in Kingston and is the author of the poetry books *Status Update* (2013), which was nominated for the Pat Lowther Award, and the Gerald Lampert Award-winning *Sweet Devilry* (2011). Her new book, *Grappling Hook,* is forthcoming with Palimpsest Press. She is the editor of the poetry collection *Desperately Seeking Susans* (2013) and the poetry editor for *Arc Poetry Magazine*.

Of "Retirement Plans," Tsiang writes: "We live in a house that is over a hundred years old and it is always acting up (lights flickering, doors opening). One day my rotary phone rang even though I had unplugged it from the telephone line. It turned my mind to my own future hauntings."

Arielle Twist is a Nehiyaw, Two-Spirit author and multidisciplinary artist originally from George Gordon First Nation, Saskatchewan, now based out of Halifax, Nova Scotia. Her debut collection, *Disintegrate/Dissociate*, won The Indigenous Voices Award for Published Poetry and the 2020 Dayne Ogilvie Prize for Emerging LGBTQ Writers. Her work has been exhibited at the Art Gallery of Mississauga, Art Gallery of Nova Scotia, and the Agnes Etherington Art Gallery. In 2019 she was awarded the Indigenous Artist Recognition Award from Arts NS for her body of work. She is currently an MFA Candidate at OCAD University.

Of "Gravel," Twist writes: "The poem was written while grieving a lover—there is no motive behind this piece, nor is there an academic or intentional reasoning behind the structure. I was consumed by this grief and it was all I could write about in 2019, so I wrote, and I grieved, and it was published."

David Ezra Wang was born on Munsee Lenape land (New Jersey), raised on Ketagalan land (Taipei), and currently studies as an uninvited guest on Musqueam land. When he's with himself, he's an artist, or a writer. When he's with others, he's a friend, a comrade, a spirit, or a stone in a river.

Of "acne, blood, and all things that flow," Wang writes, "Every word that i've meant to say, i've said with my body, my absence, my existence, my movement, yet somehow it is not received. i am not in the lacking, but i am of a void—consuming the world into a point unimaginable. i know i must be small (for now), but i feel every small part of my presence. i feel it rumbling, i feel it all."

Phoebe Wang is a first-generation Chinese-Canadian writer and educator living in Toronto/Tkaronto. Her first collection of poetry, *Admission Requirements* (McClelland & Stewart, 2017) was nominated for the Trillium Book Award. Her second collection, *Waking Occupations*, is forthcoming in 2022.

She has served as a mentor with Diaspora Dialogues and works at OCAD University as a Writing and Learning Consultant for ELL students.

Of "Self-Portrait with an Internal Conflict," Wang writes: "The poem draws upon watching my mother work on watercolour still lifes when I was growing up. She would meticulously arrange everyday objects and flowers and render them with a sense of control that awed me. That control was not only evident in her artistic practice but in the way she arranged the house and her life, as if it were on display, yet the hand that arranged them and the light source was 'unseen.' Her illustrative style resulted in work, and a world, that did not allow for flaws, messiness, or signs of 'rot or browning.' The title is somewhat ironic, because it appeared to me that she had no internal conflict in her quest for a certain aesthetic, and the painting is in fact a self-portrait of her perfectionism. In this poem the speaker refuses to romanticize the work and employs a matter-of-fact tone. With comma splices and run-on sentences, the lines mimic the flow of thinking through a problem aloud. There's a loose sonnet structure underpinning the poem, a structure I find very serviceable when writing about family. It allows for a question or position in the first half, a turn or pivot, and an answer that begins with 'and yet beauty persists.' My mother's idealized views made our ordinary world into art and filled in the blankness of arrival, but who was she persuading, herself, or us? It's a question I'm still answering."

Hayden Ward currently lives in Montreal. Ward holds an undergraduate degree from the University of British Columbia Okanagan and his gramps thinks that's pretty great. His poems have appeared in *EVENT*, *Grain*, and *Nu Lit House*.

Of "From the Nurse's Cabin Porch, Keats Island," Ward writes: "This poem comes from a series of poems I have been writing about Keats Island, an island in the Howe Sound, opposite the small township of Gibson's Landing on the unceded territory of the Squamish Nation. When I was a kid, my parents would volunteer and work at the Baptist bible camp, Keats Camps, on the westmost end of the island. I spent most of my childhood summers there, running around the island. Originally, the poem was very crowded together and was written as a single stanza. I wanted the stanza to be entrapping and to ensnare me somehow. At the time, I was reading the Robert Hass translations of Basho and was trying to write haikus. By opening up the block stanza into shapes that were following the idea of haikus, I was able to enter into the space of the poem more honestly and empathetically— able to more plainly see the landscape of my memory, of my mum, of the boy, of the hornets. The poem for me had always been one reaching towards reconciling my memory of that place: what did it mean to have grown up there? What did it mean to have memories of my mum caring for other kids? What did it mean to have spent all my childhood summers at a bible camp on an island? What does it mean to tell stories to yourself about yourself?"

Elana Wolff lives and works in Thornhill, Ontario. Elana's collection, *Swoon* (Guernica Editions), was the winner of the 2020 Canadian Jewish Literary Award for Poetry. Poems from *Swoon* can be found in *EVENT Magazine, Grain, Literary Review of Canada, Riddle Fence*, and *Room* magazine, among other places. New poems appear in *Arc Poetry Magazine, Canadian Literature, The Dalhousie Review, The Maynard, The Pi Review*, and *The The: an online journal of poem plus critique* by Catherine Owen.

Of "I Really Liked Your Reading Last Night," Wolff writes: "The poem is about a poetry reading event and feelings and ideas that bubble up for the 'I' of the title, the day after. The poem comprises eight central couplets—reflecting the two players in the piece: narrator / presenter and addressee / interlocutor. The couplets are bracketed top and bottom by two single lines, both beginning with 'You,' to indicate separateness and points of view. The opening line sets the stage: 'You came alone and sat at the back of the room.' The closing line strikes at the nub of what's at stake; namely, what is felt by the teller (poetry pivots on feeling) and how the telling is told (poetry stands on craft). The word 'slant' is used twice—riffing on Emily Dickinson's famous dictum: 'Tell the truth but tell it slant,' here indicating lexical play and indirectness, and ambiguity of feeling. Is truth a kind of earnestness? Is metaphor a kind of irony? Can the writer really only bring a monopolized point of view? This poem wrangles with these questions."

Eugenia Zuroski is an American of Chinese, Italian, and Polish descent currently living in Dish with One Spoon territory (Hamilton, Ontario). She is the author of the chapbook *Hovering, Seen* (Anstruther Press, 2019) and her poems have appeared in *Columba* and *Room*. Zuroski teaches literature and critical theory in the Department of English and Cultural Studies at McMaster University and is editor of the scholarly journal *Eighteenth-Century Fiction*, published by University of Toronto Press.

Of "a wing on the pavement, now kept in a jar," Zuroski writes: "This poem belongs to a cluster of pieces I sketched in a notebook in 2018, on days I found myself walking and riding the bus through downtown Hamilton with my daughter, who was then six years old. I was documenting the rhythm and content of our conversations, which compelled me to pay attention to things 'as they are' in an up-to-the-moment way. The title is both a metaphor for the way we collect pieces of the world through such practices of observation and documentation—one meant to call attention to the intertwined dynamics of mystery, beauty, and violence in acts of collection—and a reference to an actual starling wing that my daughter once found on the sidewalk, which now sits in a jar in our dining room."

Jan Zwicky grew up in the northwest corner of the Great Central Plain on Treaty 6 territory, was educated at the universities of Calgary and Toronto, and currently lives on Canada's west coast in unceded territory with a complex history including Coast Salish and Kwakwaka'wakw influences. Her most recent book, a collection of essays, is *The Experience of Meaning*.

Of "Learning to Die," Zwicky writes: "Northrop Frye said: 'The fact that revision is possible, that the poet makes changes not because [the poet] likes them better but because they *are* better, means that poems . . . are born not made. The poet's task is to deliver the poem in as uninjured a state as possible, and if the poem is alive, it is equally anxious to be rid of [the poet], and screams to be cut loose from [their] private memories and associations, [their] desire for self-expression, [etc.]' ('The Archetypes of Literature,' §VII of My Credo: A Symposium of Critics, *Kenyon Review*, XII.1: 97, my italics.) I think Northrop Frye is right, and his account helps us understand why it is a matter of justice and respect to let poems speak for themselves."

NOTABLE POEMS OF 2020

Chris Banks
"Honeydripper"
The Malahat Review 211

Moni Brar
"Test Case"
Freefall #2

Michelle Poirier Brown
"A Perspective on
Women"
Arc Poetry Magazine 92

Sadiqa de Meijer
"Incantation"
The Walrus
April 2020

Jean Eng
"Missing a Father"
Ricepaper Magazine
June 2020

Whitney French
"Long Night"
Arc Poetry Magazine 92

Izza Hassan
"Jet Lagged"
Contemporary Verse 2

Bára Hladik
"Telephone"
Event 49.2

Evan J
"Another Death at the
Learning Centre"
SubTerrain 86

Gary Lai
"A Lament About Opec"
The Goose Vol. 18, No. 2

Tess Liem
  "A Request"
  Boston Review

Natalie Lim
  "conversations with
  mom"
  Room 42.4

Lillian Necakov
  "8"
  SubTerrain 87

David O'Meara
  "Autobiography"
  The Walrus
  March 2020

Alexandra Oliver
  "Best Practice"
  The Walrus
  March 2020

Dominik Parisien
  "Make Your Poems
  Voyagers"
  Event 49.2

Terese Mason Pierre
  "Fishing"
  Brick 106

Alycia Pirmohamed
  "Meditation While
  Plaiting My Hair"
  Vida Review #3

Shazia Hafiz Ramji
  "Dear Kin"
  Event 49.3

Kulbir Saran
  "unsaid"
  The Malahat Review 209

Bardia Sinaee
  "Triptych"
  The Puritan 50

Katie Thompson
  "I need another new day"
  Arc Poetry Magazine 93

Elaine van der Geld
  "Overpass"
  Contemporary Verse 2
  Summer 2020

Sarah Venart
  "Denouement"
  The Malahat Review 211

Melissa Spohr Weiss
  "Gift in German Means
  Poison"
  The Malahat Review 211

Patricia Young
  "Interpretation"
  Prairie Fire Vol. 41, No. 4

Changming Yuan
  "Musings over
  Metamorphosis"
  Ricepaper Magazine
  March 2020

MAGAZINES CONSULTED

Each year, the fifty best poems and the list of notable poems by Canadian poets are selected from more than sixty print and online journals published in the previous year. While direct submissions of individual poems are not accepted, we welcome review copies from print outlets and announcements of new issues from online publications. Please direct two copies of each print issue to Best Canadian Poetry c/o Biblioasis, 1686 Ottawa St, Ste 100, Windsor, ON N8Y 1R1, or email us at bestcanadianpoetry@biblioasis.com.

The Antigonish Review (antigonishreview.com). PO Box 5000, Antigonish, NS, B2G 2W5

Arc Poetry Magazine (arcpoetry.ca). PO Box 81060, Ottawa, ON, K1P 1B1

Brick, A Literary Journal (brickmag.com). PO Box 609, Stn. P, Toronto, ON, M5S 2Y4

Bywords (bywords.ca)

Canadian Broadcasting Corporation, CBC Poetry Prize finalists (cbc.ca)

Canadian Literature (canlit.ca). University of British Columbia, 8–6303 NW Marine Dr., Vancouver, BC, V6T 1Z1

Canadian Notes & Queries (notesandqueries.ca).1686 Ottawa
    St., Suite 100, Windsor, ON N8Y 1R1.

Canthius (canthius.com)

The Capilano Review (thecapilanoreview.ca). 102-281 Indus-
    trial Ave., Vancouver, BC, V6A 2P2

Carousel (carouselmagazine.ca). UC 274, University of Guelph,
    Guelph, ON, N1G 2W1

Carte Blanche (carte-blanche.org)

Cascadia Rising Review (cascadiarisingreview.com)

Contemporary Verse 2 (*CV2*) (contemporaryverse2.ca). 502–
    100 Arthur St., Winnipeg, MB, R3B 1H3

Cosmonauts Avenue (cosmonautsavenue.com)

Dalhousie Review (dalhousiereview.dal.ca). Dalhousie Uni-
    versity, Halifax, NS, B3H 4R2

Dusie (dusie.org)

EVENT (eventmagazine.ca). PO Box 2503, New Westminster,
    BC, V3L 5B2

Exile Quarterly (theexilewriters.com). Exile/Excelsior Pub-
    lishing Inc., 170 Wellington St. W, PO Box 308, Mount
    Forest, ON, N0G 2L0

Existere (yorku.ca/existere). Vanier College 101E, York Uni-
    versity, 4700 Keele St., Toronto, ON, M3J 1P3

Feathertale (feathertale.com/review). PO Box 5023, Ottawa,
    ON, K2C 3H3

The Fiddlehead (thefiddlehead.ca). Campus House, Univer-
    sity of New Brunswick, 11 Garland Ct., PO Box 4400,
    Fredericton, NB, E3B 5A3

filling Station (fillingstation.ca). PO Box 22135, Bankers Hall,
    Calgary, AB, T2P 4J5

Forget Magazine (orgetmagazine.com). 810–1111, Melville St.,
    Vancouver, BC, V6E 3V6

Geist (geist.com). Suite 210, 111 W. Hastings St., Vancouver,
    BC, V6B 1H4

Glass Buffalo (glassbuffalo.com). HC 3–59, Humanities Build-
    ing, University of Alberta, 116 St. and 85 Ave., Edmonton,
    AB, TG6 2R3

Grain (grainmagazine.ca). PO Box 3986, Regina, SK, S4P 3R9

HA&L (Hamilton Arts & Letters Magazine) (halmagazine. wordpress.com)

Juniper (juniperpoetry.com)

The Leaf (brucedalepress.ca). PO Box 2259, Port Elgin, ON, N0H 2C0

Lemon Hound (lemonhound.com)

The Literary Review of Canada (reviewcanada.ca). *340 King St E, Toronto, ON M5A 1K8*

Maisonneuve (maisonneuve.org). 1051 boul. Decarie, PO Box 53527, Saint Laurent, QC, H4L 5J9

The Malahat Review (malahatreview.ca). University of Victoria, PO Box 1700, Stn. CSC, Victoria, BC, V8W 2Y2

Maple Tree Literary Supplement (mtls.ca). 1103–1701 Kilborn Ave., Ottawa, ON, K1H 6M8

The Maynard (themaynard.org)

Minola Review (minolareview.ca)

The Nashwaak Review (www.stu.ca/english/the-nashwaak-review/). St. Thomas University, Fredericton, NB, E3B 5G3

New Poetry (newpoetry.ca)

The New Quarterly (tnq.ca). St. Jerome's University, 290 Westmount Rd. N, Waterloo, ON, N2L 3G3

The New Yorker (newyorker.com/fiction-and-poetry). 1 World Trade Center, New York, NY, USA, 10007

Newfoundland Quarterly (nqonline.ca). E 4001, Memorial University, St. John's, NL, A1C 5S7

ottawater (ottawater.com)

Poem-a-Day (poets.org/poem-a-day). Academy of American Poets, 75 Maiden Lane, Suite 901, New York, NY, USA, 10038

Poetry Magazine (poetryfoundation.org/poetrymagazine). 61 West Superior St., Chicago, IL, USA, 60654

Poetry Is Dead (poetryisdead.ca). 5020 Frances St., Burnaby, BC, V5B 1T3

Poetry Pause (poets.ca/poetrypause/). League of Canadian Poets, 2 Carleton St., Suite 1519, Toronto, ON, M5B 1J3

Prairie Fire (prairiefire.ca). 423–100 Arthur St., Winnipeg, MB, R3B 1H3

PRISM international (prismmagazine.ca). Creative Writing Program, University of British Columbia, Buchanan Room E462, 1866 Main Mall, Vancouver, BC, V6T 1Z1

The Puritan (puritan-magazine.com)

Queen's Quarterly (queensu.ca/quarterly). Queen's University, 144 Barrie St., Kingston, ON, K7L 3N6

Ricepaper Magazine (ricepapermagazine.ca). PO Box 74174, Hillcrest RPO, Vancouver, BC, V5V 5L8

Riddle Fence (riddlefence.com)

Room (roommagazine.com). PO Box 46160, Stn. D, Vancouver, BC, V6J 5G5

subTerrain (subterrain.ca). PO Box 3008, MPO, Vancouver, BC, V6B 3X5

Taddle Creek (taddlecreekmag.com). PO Box 611, Stn. P, Toronto, ON, M5S 2Y4

The / temz / Review (thetemzreview.com)

This Magazine (this.org). 417–401 Richmond St. W, Toronto, ON, M5V 3A8

Understory (understorymagazine.ca). RR#1, Lunenburg, NS, B0J 2C0

Vallum (vallummag.com). 5038 Sherbrooke W., PO Box 23077, CP Vendome, Montreal, QC, H4A 1T0

The Walrus (walrusmagazine.com). 411 Richmond St. E., Suite B15, Toronto, ON, M5A 3S5

West End Phoenix (westendphoenix.com). The Gladstone Hotel, 1214 Queen St. W., Toronto, ON, M6J 1J6

White Wall Review (whitewallreview.com). Department of English: 10th floor Jorgenson Hall, Ryerson University, 350 Victoria Street, Toronto, ON, M5B 2K3

ACKNOWLEDGEMENTS

"a wing on the pavement, now kept in a jar" appeared in *Room* copyright © Eugenia Zuroski. Reprinted with permission of the author.

"acne, blood, and all things that flow" appeared in *Ricepaper Magazine* copyright © David Ezra Wang. Reprinted with permission of the author.

"All clear" appeared in *Arc Poetry Magazine* copyright © Maureen Hynes. Reprinted with permission of the author.

"an ode to my brother's forehead stitches" appeared in *Room* copyright © Unnati Desai. Reprinted with permission of the author.

"Another Woman in Canada" appeared in *Geist* copyright © George K Ilsley. Reprinted with permission of the author.

"Asch's Line Study in the Current Anthropocene" appeared in *Grain* copyright © Paola Ferrante. Reprinted with permission of the author.

"Attention" appeared in *Grain* copyright © Kate Cayley. Reprinted with permission of the author.

INDEX TO POETS

EDITOR BIOGRAPHIES

Souvankham Thammavongsa is the author of five books: *Small Arguments* (2003), winner of the ReLit Prize; *Found* (2007), now a short film; *Light* (2013), winner of the Trillium Book Award for Poetry; *Cluster* (2019); and the short story collection *How to Pronounce Knife* (2020), winner of the Scotiabank Giller prize and Trillium Book Award, and a *New York Times* Editors' Choice. She has been in residence at Yaddo and has presented her poetry at the Guggenheim Museum in New York.

Anita Lahey's latest book is *The Last Goldfish: a True Tale of Friendship* (Biblioasis, 2020). A poet, journalist, essayist, she's also the author of *The Mystery Shopping Cart: Essays on Poetry and Culture* (Palimpsest, 2013), and two Véhicule Press poetry collections: *Spinning Side Kick* and *Out to Dry in Cape Breton*. The latter was shortlisted for the Trillium Book Award for Poetry and the Ottawa Book Award. Anita's magazine journalism has received several National Magazine Award honourable mentions. Anita grew up in Burlington, Ontario; has lived in Toronto, Montreal, Fredericton and Victoria; and has close family ties to Cape Breton Island. She now lives in Ottawa, on unceded Alongonquin, Anishinabek territory, with her family and their little black cat, Milli.